INSPIRATION UNIVERSAL AND UNLIMITED

Motivation Scatters; Inspiration Gathers

INSPIRATION
UNIVERSAL AND UNLIMITED

Motivation Scatters; Inspiration Gathers

ROGER W. STEINKRUGER

STONE SIEL PRESS

First Edition: May 2022
Printed in the United States of America

979-8-9860576-0-6 - Hardcover edition
979-8-9860576-1-3 - Paperback edition
979-8-9860576-2-0 - eBook edition
979-8-9860576-3-7 - Audiobook

STONE SIEL PRESS

DEDICATION

This book is dedicated to several individuals within my inner circle.

To Nancy—high school sweetheart, first love of my life, and wife, whose death was unexpected—for not only her unwavering love, but her encouragement to write this book. In Nancy's absence, I honor my mother-in-law, Velma, who continues to love and treat me as her own son, and;

To Mary Lou—the second love of my life and my wife—for her unconditional love and reassurance to fulfill this dream of writing this book—and for filling my heart again, and;

To our children, Natalie, Matt, David, and son-in-law Kirk, for their love, respect, and encouragement. They embellish our lives in many ways, and finally;

To our grandchildren, Kensington (Kensi) and Graham for their endearing love and insatiable appetites for learning and experiencing new things—and for making us proud grandparents.

CONTENTS

FOREWORD

George Bernard Shaw wrote, "Those who can, do, those who can't teach." Roger Steinkruger is one who has been a "do" person all his life, and this gives him the unique qualifications and experience to teach—and teach he does in *"Inspiration Universal and Unlimited...Motivation Scatters; Inspiration Gathers".* So many teachers of leadership and personal development are better at teaching than actually "doing." Roger Steinkruger is not one of them.

The resulting wisdom you will find in this book—a hybrid between memoir and a user-manual for life—is the result of Roger's living and teaching principles and behaviors that have inspired hundreds and built great organizations. Rarely are we fortunate to learn from a practitioner who is also a great teacher. It has been my honor to have collaborated with Roger, and to have enjoyed a lasting kinship together, a bond that resulted from bearing witness to Roger's spirit-centered way of living and leading.

What you will also enjoy, beyond this spirit-centered wisdom and practical experience, is the humility and vulnerability that Roger brings to these pages. This is not a "I-was-a-wonderful-leader-and-I-am-going-to-show-you-how-you-can-be-too" book. As Roger states himself, he is an imperfect human being, like all of us, and this makes the wisdom contained here utterly relatable.

The key to making this world a better place is to become inspired and to be inspiring—everywhere. A loving heart (inspirational) will always triumph over a fear-based one (motivational). While motivation is effective in the short term, it is inspiration that more effectively sustains long-term change and growth. We have become exceptionally good at motivating, but we have not yet written the playbook for inspiration—most people couldn't even tell the difference. Everywhere in our lives we have honed our fear-based communications and actions—in politics, international relations, marketing and advertising, parenting, religion, law enforcement, academia, healthcare, entertainment, media, and more. We know how to use the carrot (inducement) or the stick (punishment) in all of these different arenas, but we have yet to learn how to inspire. How do you close a factory in a way that inspires everyone? How do you end an employee's job so that they feel inspired, not motivated? How do you negotiate for peace by inspiring instead of threatening? This is where life becomes challenging, and this is the nuanced message that Roger has created to reveal the different approaches needed.

You will find the integration of work and life a key part of Roger's message—there is no separation between work and life—they are one. Work is just one aspect of life. There are powerful examples of this idea throughout this book, which reinforces the notion that we can only have one kind of behavior in our lives if we wish to be inspired and to inspire others. We don't just tell the truth at home and then lie, steal, and cheat at work. We are the same souls in every environment, and you will find in these pages ways to live inspiring principles across your whole life. To quote Mahatma Gandhi, "One man cannot do right in one department of life whilst he is occupied in doing wrong in any other department. Life is one indivisible whole."

Roger writes, "Go out of your way to make bigger those who are made to feel small and the big, no bigger than they are." The wisdom in these pages will make every reader feel bigger, and help the reader to inspire others, making them "bigger" too.

Lance Secretan, PhD
Best-selling Author, Voted Top 30 Leadership Experts and Coaches in the World
Founder and CEO, The Secretan Center, Inc.

PREFACE

I hope you will read this book cover to cover, especially the preface prior to turning to the heart of the book.

One of the premises of my life and this book, is that I strive to live as one individual, not three: as (1) a spouse or significant other, parent, family member, (2) an employee, and (3) a citizen of community, state, and country. I refer to these three as spheres. In this world of trials and tribulations, it is difficult to live and survive as one individual, let alone as three individuals in one body.

Many of us believe (or live as though we believe) we must maintain three or more distinct sets of beliefs and values, behave differently in each of these spheres, and perform specifically to the norms of each sphere to be considered successful (and be accepted).

To maintain these multiple sets of belief and values, we often leave carnage behind, strewn across the paths we chose. Examples of such carnage may be classified by the sphere in which it occurs as (1) *family:* broken marriages, shared or no parental custody, strained or severed family relationships, (2) *employment:* poor employee morale, lack of employee-employer trust, strained employee relationships, fired employees, mass layoffs, employee litigation against employers, high employee turnover, high replacement costs, low productivity, and (3) *citizen:* lack of respect for public servants, broken community promises, unemployment, community passivity, lack of confidence in elected officials, reduced literacy rates, community violence.

It is not my purpose to address social ills identified as a citizen. I will focus on the relationship between family and employment life. If family and employment become congruent, *community* will be addressed through the alignment of the first two spheres.

This book will focus on employment life. The intended audience includes (1) CEOs, (2) leadership team members, (3) management staff, (4) individuals who are aspiring to leadership roles at all levels, (5) existing staff who want to contribute to a more inspirational, loving culture, and (6) individuals who are seeking employment in high performing, inspirational organizations.

With over fifty years of experience in healthcare, and twenty-five as a hospital CEO, I have learned many practical suggestions which I hope to share with you to enhance your personal and professional life and save pain and suffering at home and at work.

I am reminded of *The Starfish Story,* by Loren Eiseley:

> One day, a man was walking along the beach when he noticed a boy picking something up and gently throwing it into the ocean. Approaching the boy, he asked, "What are you doing?" The youth replied, "Throwing starfish back into the ocean. The surf is up and the tide is going out. If I don't throw them back, they'll die." "Son," the man said, "don't you realize there are miles and miles of beach and hundreds of starfish? You can't make a difference!" After listening politely, the boy bent down, picked up another starfish, and threw it back into the surf. Then smiling at the man, he said, "I made a difference for that one."

Accordingly I renew my commitment to making a difference, even if it is only for a few or just one.

I believe we need to live our lives as one individual—not two, three, or more—and therefore I wish you to know me for what and where I have been, who and where I am today, and understand my personal journey. I refer to this as *My Story*. We all have stories. Each of you have *Your Story*, as well. Sharing our stories is a unique gift we can give to one another, as we have so much to learn from each another.

I have always enjoyed movies. If I miss the first few minutes of a movie, I can fail to understand the characters, which can spoil the story line. I need first to know the characters—their backgrounds, the circumstances of their roles, and their relationships with one another. I can ask someone else "What have I missed?" This may be helpful, but now I am relying on someone else's impressions, rather than my own, and I risk not properly connecting characters to plot. And so it is here, as I share *My Story.*

This book is not an autobiography. However, If you know me you will better appreciate my message. I want you to be familiar with a light smattering of my early family life, upbringing, education, work experiences, hobbies, beliefs, values, principles, personal convictions, what is important to me, and a *few* of my shortcomings, so you can better appreciate my purpose and message. If you know what makes me tick, you will better appreciate the chiming of my clock, and its utilitarian value in marking time and purpose.

One of the first things to know about me are my priorities. My *first* priority is my faith, to my Lord and Savior, Jesus Christ—*my very best friend.* My *second* priority is my family—my wife, *my very best friend on earth,* our children and grandchildren—and work is my *third* priority. My *fourth* priority is the social and community aspects of life.

I share this so you will better understand why the beginning of this book is about *Spiritual Beliefs and Underpinnings.* My purpose is not to influence you, but to help you better understand me and the purpose of this book through my personal experiences and convictions.

The second thing to know about me is I am an imperfect human being. Quite a revelation, do you agree? In spite of my best intentions, I have not always been consistent in aligning my priorities as depicted above.

A third thing to know about me is that, although I have lived a blessed life, I am also familiar with loss. In addition to losing both of my parents and four grandparents, my first wife (Nancy) and I experienced the loss of a still-born son, followed by several miscarriages before being blessed with two healthy sons.

My greatest personal loss was Nancy's sudden and unexpected death at the young age of sixty-four years, instantly shattering so many hopes and dreams. Nancy was my high school sweetheart and the first love of my life.

I have since remarried, to a college friend shared by both Nancy and me—Mary Lou is the second love of my life. I often muse that God has blessed me with two loving wives, both patient enough to not only tolerate my imperfections but to help me improve upon my shortcomings. Through our marriage, in addition to my two great sons, Mary Lou and I now have a beautiful daughter, an upstanding son-in-law, and two loving grandchildren. God has been good.

The fourth thing to know about me is I have experienced and addressed almost every conceivable work-related set of circumstances and challenges one can imagine. I often say, "There is always a little good in what appears to be the worst at the time." This optimistic attitude has served me well and contributed to my learning.

While these aspects suggest what the book is about, it is equally important to tell you what the book is not about. This is not another *leadership model,* written for the purpose of promoting one more synthetic approach to *leadership.* Rather, it is a collection of practical suggestions and recommendations, which if adopted with sincerity, will make it easier to master the leadership model with roots in the beginning of time: *Inspiring, Loving, Servant Leadership.*

If I were to select two professional regrets, it would be these, which are linked:

1) I regret being caught up in the hype of numerous leadership models and investing so much time, money, and organizational wear and tear, in trying to make the latest shiny model work, on the heels of those that had previously failed miserably. If only I had invested the same amount of time and resources in becoming a more inspiring, loving, servant leader—at home and at work. But, "It is never too late to do the right thing."

    These *flavors of the month* leadership models only treat the symptoms, not the disease.
2) My second regret is that I did not share my own beliefs with others, earlier in my career.

I will always credit Lance Secretan, PhD, internationally-renowned author, speaker, and friend, for permitting me and countless others to become comfortable and confident in promoting (and practicing) *inspiration* rather than *motivation*; loving others as ourselves in the work place, and the power of serving others versus being served by others. *It is never too late to do the right thing.*

Many of my suggestions and recommendations in this book are my own, while others have been borrowed or adapted. I sincerely hope you will discover and create new insights or affirmations of your own. Most of all, my desire is that you will find the same gratification I have found in promoting and inspiring positive changes in the personal and professional lives of others. Collecting from the past and paying forward is a powerful force.

While running errands one day, I had convinced myself I deserved a little "pick me up" treat. I found myself driving out of my way to a favorite drive-through restaurant. As I snaked my way through the string of cars in the drive-through lane, I continued to question whether or not this calling was a need or a want. As I drove away from the window with my beverage and snack, it became crystal clear to me.

I had just turned through the last bend in the line of cars as I approached the pay window, when I took special note of the car behind me in my side mirror. It was a clean, older car with considerable exterior wear and tear. Behind the wheel, barely visible over the dashboard, was an elderly, pleasant-looking lady. Why had I taken special note of this lady? Maybe it was because I sensed that life had been difficult for her.

As I approached the pay window, I told the cashier to add the older lady's tab to my own. I immediately found myself being pretty pumped-up about my *paying it forward* deed for the day. After all, I had just reached deep into my pocket and paid for a *two for one* fish sandwich, a small single burger, and a dollar-drink, all for a grand total of $6.84, including tax.

As I drove away, I could not resist watching the two actors at the pay window—the cashier and the older lady. The scene as it unfolded was most humbling to me. A small outreached hand from the car was met mid-air with the extended hand of the cashier. She had obviously paid for the car behind her. The odds are she paid more for the car behind her, than I had paid for her meager lunch. I was no longer pumped-up about what I had done, but I was inspired with what she had done. Maybe it was a result of my example, or perhaps, she made a regular practice of performing this very gesture.

And so it is with me and this book. I will be gratified if you are inspired with even the slightest of these recommendations but, I will really be inspired in trusting that you, in turn, will inspire others at home and at work and positively influence the lives of many.

Roger W. Steinkruger
April 2022

ACKNOWLEDGMENTS

It is said, "It takes a village to raise a child." I believe, "It takes several villages *(organizations)* and many villagers *(family members, employees, and others)* to write and publish a book focused on life-long experiences, culminating in my practical suggestions and recommendations for becoming an inspiring, loving, servant leader at home and at work.

Individuals and family from my youth, those I have worked with, and others I have interacted with in various capacities, have influenced who I am today and impacted my qualifications to write and share this book with you. The vast majority of these interactions have been positive, while a very small number have been negative. I have learned from both—and I express my gratitude to all.

Many of you are referenced in my book, *Inspiration Universal and Unlimited…Motivation Scatters; Inspiration Gathers.* I have identified and honored several of my mentors throughout the book. This is in keeping with one of the sections in my book entitled, "Recognize Mentors While They Are Still Living". I remain grateful to each of you, as mentor and friend, for your contributions in making me a better person.

I acknowledge, honor, and thank Lance Secretan PhD, as teacher, mentor, and personal friend for his knowledge, expertise, and encouragement. Lance is an internationally renowned author, speaker, consultant, and advisor to many. He lives and shares his life as a model of an inspiring, loving, servant leader—practicing what he professes.

I am grateful to Phil Whitmarsh, my navigator at Redbrush, for his creativity, assistance, and support throughout the various stages of writing and publishing *Inspiration Universal and Unlimited... Motivation Scatters; Inspiration Gathers.*

I remain indebted to each of you individually, and all of you collectively, for your love and inspiration. Thanks for your unique contributions in enriching and blessing my life.

Roger ("Rog") W. Steinkruger

INTRODUCTION

If your actions inspire others to dream more, learn more, do more and become more, you are a leader.

—John Quincy Adams

This quote, by John Quincy Adams, is inscribed on a 20 in. x 26 in. wooden placard that hangs prominently on one of the walls of my office and study. The words, *inspire, dream, learn, become,* and *leader* are emboldened. This was one of the retirement gifts I received from the leadership team that had been a tremendous blessing to me for the last five-plus years of my career as a hospital CEO.

I was fortunate in having several primary and secondary school teachers who not only encouraged good writing skills but were adamant I do my best in meeting their standards. Miss Geiselman, my high school English teacher, was a strict lady of few words, but she insisted on perfection in spelling, grammar, sentence structure, and literature interpretation. Ironically, she devoted her entire life to words—and the inspiration thereof. To the credit of these teachers, I developed a lifelong interest in and appreciation for writing. I found words to be important and powerful in conveying meaning and emotion. Words can hammer the hardiest of nails and soften the hardest of steel alloys.

Early in my married and professional life, I established a goal to one day focus on writing—other than what was required with my work. You have been introduced to Nancy, the first love of my life. Nancy was the only person I shared this ambition with initially; and throughout our years together, I would reaffirm it from time to time. When we discussed it, I predictably would say, (1) I do not know what I will write about, and (2) I will think more about it when we start planning for retirement. Nancy would always add her words of encouragement.

In the weeks following Nancy's untimely death, as I was sorting through her personal affects, I found a cherished gift-to-be from Nancy. Tucked away, she had hidden a hardback copy of *Freedom*, a novel by Jonathan Franzen. Inside the front cover was a personalized pre-retirement card for me. This was my sign, my impetus to pursue my dream. Regarding subject matter, it became clear to me I should focus on the years of experiences we had shared, personally and professionally. Mary Lou, the second love of my life, has been an inspiration to me through her ongoing support and encouragement toward fulfilling my dream.

Throughout this book, I reference and honor mentors who have impacted my life. Some of these individuals have been present during most of my personal life. Other relationships solidified as our professional paths crossed and converged for periods of time, traveling together, weaving in and out of life's traffic. I look forward to introducing Mr. Lance Secretan, PhD, as one of these individuals who is prominently named on both of my personal and professional listings. Lance continues to be a blessing in my life.

Many of the tenets in this book are rooted in the merits of inspiration in our personal and professional lives. I appreciate the differentiation Lance strikes between motivation and inspiration: *Motivation* is lighting a fire *under* someone, and *Inspiration* is lighting a fire *within* someone. I find these differences polarizing in application through our lives.

With Lance's permission, I have structured my book in partial alignment with portions of his book; entitled, *The Spark, the Flame, and the Torch . . . Inspire Self. Inspire Others. Inspire the World.* Following is an abbreviated outline of my book, which will be helpful in connecting major chapters, all centering on *the fire within:*

Gathering: *The Tinder and Kindling*
Igniting: *The Spark . . . Inspire Self*
Stoking: *The Fire with Wood*
Fanning: *The Flame . . . Inspire Others*
Lighting: *The Torch . . . Inspire the World*
Refueling: *The Souls and Organizations of the World*

I have entitled my book, *Inspiration Universal and Unlimited . . . Motivation Scatters; Inspiration Gathers.* This book is a compilation of practical suggestions and recommendations, amplified with personal stories, and written for an intended audience of: (1) CEOs, (2) leadership team members, (3) management staff, (4) individuals who are aspiring to leadership roles at all levels, (5) existing staff who want to contribute to a more inspirational, loving culture, and (6) individuals who are seeking employment in high performing, inspirational organizations.

This book has three primary premises: First, we should be the same person at home and at work; Second, inspiration (being love-based), unites and gathers and motivation (being fear-based), divides and scatters; and the Third premise focuses on the virtues associated with inspiring, loving, servant leadership. All three premises lie within the overarching auspice, "Inspiration applies to everyone and is endless in degree and amount," as captured in its title, *Inspiration Universal and Unlimited . . . Motivation Scatters; Inspiration Gathers.*

Following is a synopsis of each chapter, listed above:

Gathering: *The Tinder and Kindling*
This chapter focuses on the substances I have found necessary

in my own life to build a fire within: selected Spiritual Beliefs and Underpinnings and principles associated with Inspiration versus Motivation.

Igniting: *The Spark . . . Inspire Self*

This chapter includes twenty-eight practical suggestions and recommendations to inspire oneself and—in preparation for what lies beyond—to inspire others.

Stoking: *The Fire with Wood*

In this chapter, I elaborate on three experiences that occurred early in my career but positively affected (stoked) my entire career.

Fanning: *The Flame . . . Inspire Others*

This chapter, which includes thirty-two practical suggestions and recommendations, is designed to help you utilize everything that has inspired you, as discussed within ***Igniting:*** *The Spark,* to now inspire those around you—specifically, those you will depend upon to inspire the entire organization.

Lighting: *The Torch . . . Inspire the World*

This chapter, which includes eight practical suggestions and recommendations, will prove helpful in positioning your organization as a humble, shining example of how an organization comprised of inspiring, loving, servants and servant leaders treats its employees; fulfills personal and organizational dreams; functions as a strong, engaged corporate citizen; and returns more to the world than it extracts.

Refueling: *The Souls and Organizations of the World*

This chapter reaffirms the purpose and application of this book as we contemplate required adjustments in our places of work, as influenced by coronavirus. More than ever before, all of us will be called upon to be inspiring, loving, servants and servant leaders, in refueling the souls within our own organizations, along with others within our states, across this country, and globally throughout the world. We are reminded, we are all *in* this together—and *for* one another."

GATHERING THE TINDER AND KINDLING

Spiritual Beliefs and Underpinnings

1) **God-incidence; Not Coincidence and Blessed; Not Lucky**

I have come to believe that God, being a sovereign God, has His hands on everything that occurs and with perfect timing. I am not capable of understanding how all of this happens; however, through faith and a trusting relationship with Him, I do believe He is fully capable of balancing everything universally with impeccable orchestration.

There are two words, I try to avoid using. First, using the word *coincidence* or any derivative of it, implies all things are very random without specific order and occasionally, just by chance, two or more situations will occur that appear to have a direct relationship at the time. I prefer to call these *God-incidences,* which implies specific purpose and order.

I have become so sensitized to these two words that whenever I hear either being used, it's like a little bell rings in my head and I am very apt to momentarily become distracted and not fully appreciate the message being conveyed.

The second, is the word *lucky*. I try to avoid using this word or any of its derivatives as I believe it too implies something good has happened to us by happenstance, without specific purpose or order. Instead of *luck*, I prefer *blessing;* and instead of *lucky,* I prefer *blessed.* I not only believe God blesses individuals, but I also believe He blesses organizations.

In addition to the reasons cited above, I like to use *God-incidence* and *blessing* because these words remind me to be humble in my personal accomplishments, as well as those of the organization I was responsible for at the time. It is also a gesture through which I honor my Lord.

I am also hoping by using these terms to send a similar message to those around us, whether it be staff members or community members, that we are humbling ourselves before our Maker. In an interesting twist, it makes us appear strong, rather than weak and confident, rather than boastful.

God-incidence is a bit more cumbersome to say, but I encourage the reader to become comfortable in using *blessing* and *blessed.* Instead of saying *God-incidence,* I will often describe the circumstances as a *God-thing,* accomplishing what I believe, is the same result.

As a testament to the validity of my convictions, how many times have you said, or heard others say something to the effect, *"In looking back on a particular situation, it makes much more sense now"* or *"I can see now that God had His hand on the specific circumstances"* or *"I certainly did not understand at the time; now I can see how I was being protected"*?

I could site several situations in my life where retrospect has convinced me that God had indeed protected me and my family. After all of these years, I can quickly relive the emotion attached to what happened in the early morning of that late-night drive.

It was during December of 1993. Our oldest son was three years old and my wife, unbeknown to us at the time, was pregnant with our second son. I had completed my master's degree (later in life) and I had accepted my first hospital CEO position. My wife, son, and I had the privilege of celebrating these accomplishments with a well-deserved family vacation in Phoenix, Arizona. It was an extra bonus to escape the harsh Midwest winter weather and literally bathe in the sunshine of the southwest! While there, we also planned an adjunct two-day trip from Phoenix to San Diego, to visit a cousin we had not seen for several years. The plan called for us to make the six-hour drive one day, spend the night in San Diego, and drive back the following day. The entire trip included interstate driving, taking the same route to San Diego and back again the following day. We planned to drive to San Diego leisurely, particularly with a three-year-old onboard. Our route called for us to take Interstate 10 from Phoenix south to Interstate 8 on into San Diego.

As we were driving west on Interstate 8, we commented on what appeared to be a sizable community approximately four to five miles north of I-8, shortly after we turned onto I-8. We were no doubt noting this as a place for services, if needed; especially given that we were traveling with our three-year old son.

Our drive to San Diego was uneventful. My cousin had a fun-packed itinerary planned for the four of us, including time at his home and the beach the first afternoon, several hours at Sea World the second day, along with lunches and dinners at unique restaurants both days.

Admittedly, it was hard to leave the second day, as the time had passed quickly and we were having so much fun. We needed to be back on the morning of the third day, so we compromised by staying longer than planned before leaving on our six-hour drive back to Phoenix. After all, our son would most likely sleep the entire way, given how tired he was at the end of our busy day. For this reason, we planned to make the return trip without stopping. It was approximately 8:00 P.M. before we left San Diego.

Again, our drive back to Phoenix was proving to be uneventful, and My wife and I were enjoying our time together, especially our uninterrupted time to discuss all of our upcoming changes, which included my first CEO position, listing/selling our house, purchasing a home in our new community, and all the other details of moving our family.

The memory of the events remains surreal today, even as I share this with you. Suddenly, we found ourselves driving on a two-lane highway, approaching the late-night lights of a community lying to the left of Interstate 8. We remembered looking at each other, both of us puzzled on how and why this had happened. The very first business we approached at the edge of the city was an all-night gas and convenience store. Still puzzled, we agreed that since the store was so close, we could take turns with one of us purchasing a snack and using the restroom, while the other stayed in the car with our son.

Our unplanned stop consumed approximately twenty minutes with another ten minutes needed to find our way back to Interstate 8.

After driving for approximately thirty minutes, we approached one of the worst highway accidents I have ever witnessed. It appeared that up to three cars and one semi-truck were involved in what further appeared to be head-on collisions. I believe one ambulance had just arrived with two state troopers already onsite, directing traffic and assisting with triage.

We were directed to drive on the shoulder of the road, in order to maneuver around one of the mangled cars. As we did so, we noted a body lying motionless on the highway near one of the vehicles. We learned later three people had died at the scene with another five being seriously injured. As we resumed our interstate drive, we met several other emergency vehicles on their way to the accident.

We were rather shaken with the loss of life and devastation we had just witnessed. As we pieced the timing together, we realized if we had not mysteriously been sidelined to that little town, we may have been very near, if not involved in this tragic accident.

As a result of this incident, I have two convictions: First, to this day, we truly believe God protected us that late night and that our family was not only protected, but spared. Second, I no longer become upset with the little delays and setbacks that often impact personal and professional plans, because I believe we may never know what we are being spared from in the busyness of life.

2) **Seeking God's Wisdom, Rather Than the Wisdom of the World**

As a segue from the previous section, I begin this segment by reminding myself to always give God the credit and the glory for individual and organizational accomplishments. As a leader and particularly as the CEO, I have found this particularly reassuring, as I believe all things are made possible through Him and for His purpose and His glory. This has been useful in keeping me grounded and humble and has always helped me differentiate between confidence and arrogance.

The belief that all individual strengths and talents are created and instilled in each of us by God grants credibility to the above belief. Furthermore, I believe God has created each of us for very specific reasons, according to the will He has for each of us and our respective lives. God also provides us with freedom of choice.

Certainly, it is most important to recognize and credit individuals for significant accomplishments and commendable behaviors; however, we should remember the talents and skills that made those individuals successful are God-given and we should recognize the ultimate credit and glory belongs to God.

If you accept the premises I have shared above, perhaps you will also be willing to explore the admonition of this segment to seek God's wisdom rather than the so-called wisdom of the world in all circumstances. Clearly, I always encourage that we seek council from others in both our personal and professional lives; furthermore, credible council from others may be a blessing from God. God's wisdom is timeless, pure, everlasting, and tailored for our specific lives. By contrast, the so-called wisdom of the world I refer to tends to be temporal, self-serving, and based on the will of man, not on the will of God.

Some of my most challenging circumstances and regrettable decisions have come about because I was pursuing my will and not the will of God. I have many examples, but I will share just one example that is work-related and applicable to both leaders and individuals seeking employment.

This occurred early in my career as a hospital CEO. We had an opening for the chief nursing officer (CNO) position at this mid-sized healthcare organization.

An advanced practice registered nurse (APRN), who I will refer to as Beth, was on our medical staff and had practiced in that role for several years. Beth was actively involved in the community; she and her husband had four young children; she held a master's degree in nursing; she was a well-respected practitioner and employee within the organization; and generally she was described as a likeable, go-to person in the organization.

We were in the process of recruiting on a regional basis for the CNO position. Prior to initiating this recruitment effort, Beth's name had surfaced as someone that would be excellent in the CNO role. Within a short period, a small group of supportive individuals rallied her interest and encouraged her to apply. Beth was very quick to say she enjoyed what she was doing and would absolutely not have any interest in the CNO position.

I even found myself being swept-up in this effort of

convincing Beth that this was something she should pursue for the good of the organization. I personally visited with her several times, all in an effort of filling the CNO position with the perfect candidate.

After withstanding the pressure for a couple of weeks, Beth finally caved-in, applied, completed an abbreviated interview, and was quickly named our new chief nursing officer (CNO). Everyone was happy with her decision—at least for the time being.

I learned a great deal from this experience, which ultimately ended in being the worst personnel decision I have ever made. This became very difficult to unravel, which finally occurred after many hard feelings, the destruction of friendships, the loss of unity within the leadership team, degradation resulting in a highly dysfunctional department of nursing services, and the loss of a well-respected practitioner from the medical staff.

The primary problem was we were all pursuing our own wills without being respectful of Beth's will, and perhaps most importantly, one can infer it may have been inconsistent with God's will and His intended purpose for Beth's life.

From this experience, after seeking God's counsel, I have learned to not push situations beyond the point of not feeling right anymore; to be respectful of receiving a "no" or "not now" answer; and to accept that there may be underlying reasons for something "just not coming together," as intended.

3) Everyone Has (Is) a Story

I begin this section, by quoting Fred Rogers (Mister Rogers):

As human beings, our job in life is to help people realize how rare and valuable each one of us really is, that each of us has something that no one else has—or ever will have—something inside that is unique to all time. It's our job to encourage each other to discover that uniqueness and to provide ways of developing its expression.

As one considers the sanctity of life, I remind myself again that everyone is created equally in the eyes of God and possesses God-given skills and talents, and that God has anointed each of us with a specific purpose on this earth. He has accomplished all of this for each of us, and He has also provided us with freedom of choice. Interesting twist, is it not? In acknowledging all of this, I am also reminded everyone has a story, or, as implied above, everyone *is* a story.

Admittedly, I have been guilty of rushing to judgment about individuals in general—even fellow church attendees, staff members, managers, and yes, others in prominent leadership roles. I have been most disappointed in myself when I have done this without any attempt to understand their perspectives and/or life experiences and, generally speaking, their personal and professional stories—and everyone has one.

The old adage is true: *You cannot judge a book by its cover.* On a personal note, it would be like you picking this book up, glancing at the cover, perhaps skimming the preface, leafing through the pages haphazardly, and discarding it without knowing more about me, my story, and what I may have to offer.

How many times, like me, have you been surprised and maybe even embarrassed to learn the truth about someone's story; perhaps, from the storyteller directly?

Attempting to appreciate and honor someone's story needs to come about through a genuine interest, mutual respect, and it requires a willingness to share by both individuals and a comfortable dialogue. It is also important to reassure the individual sharing their story that the shared information will remain confidential.

Why is it important to appreciate the stories of others? If utilized appropriately, this is a tool that often serves as an ice-breaker early in new relationships. It may also be helpful in building relationships; doing so becomes our core business. It is a way of honoring someone else's life, their interests, and accomplishments. Often interests, talents, and experiences will be identified that will meet an organizational need; supplement, or enhance operations; or even improve individual performance.

Within the first several months of one of my CEO positions, I found myself dealing with a challenging personnel issue. Darin was a one-person support services department. He had been hired two years before I was appointed to the CEO position. Prior to his time with us, he had been employed by an independently-owned company within the same community.

Our director of human resources (HR) asked me to become involved in addressing issues surrounding Darin and his work. I learned he initially adapted well and his performance was acceptable during those early months. Prior to my joining the organization, the HR director had begun receiving complaints about his conduct, behavior, poor responsiveness, and a slippage in the quality of his work.

As a side note, Darin was a tall, muscular man in his mid-thirties who would have passed as a professional football player, most likely a tackle in my mind. (He would later tell me he had never played football, even as a child.) This provides you with a physical description of Darin. At that time, his demeanor could also be described as being intimidating. Given the fact that the entire facility relied heavily on his services, these complaints were beginning to pile on top of one another.

The HR director and I initiated progressive discipline processes with Darin after the first verbal counseling session failed to produce positive results. We had noticed some small wins in his attitude and work performance for a short period of time, only to be disappointed yet another time.

This led us to the written disciplinary step, which we all three attended. Given the severe nature of the process by this time, I had expected Darin might be somewhat contrite and perhaps, even apologetic. But, to the contrary, he was stoic and perfunctory in his responses. I made it clear this was becoming serious, and if not corrected, could lead to his termination. I was puzzled.

In the days that followed, I found myself reflecting on Darin and his situation. During the entire process, I sensed there was another Darin underneath that outer crust. I decided to have an off the record meeting with Darin for the purpose of gaining better insight and understanding. After all, Darin was not only an employee, but a husband and a father of three young children.

Darin and I met privately for almost two hours. I initiated the conversation in the humblest and most respectful approach I could muster at the time. I was honest in sharing my observation that I believed there was another Darin underneath the image he was working hard to maintain. I expressed how important he was and, as a one-person department, we needed to rely heavily on him and his talents.

I shared some of my own experiences from early in my career when I too, believed I could operate independently without regard for the feelings and reactions of others—and most importantly, what I learned about myself and my need to change. I also expressed my desire to support him in making these needed changes for him to become successful in our organization.

This approach proved to be disarming and, before long, Darin was telling me his life's story. In that short period of time, I witnessed what I had perceived as a hard man being transformed into a humble, contrite, nearly broken man. I would learn how he had come to believe the organization did not follow through on commitments made by and during the previous CEO's tenure. This was the primary reason Darin had found himself deteriorating in character and attitude. He expressed a sincere desire to make the needed changes, and that was the most important outcome.

We would visit several times on a follow-up basis. I will spare many of the finer details of our conversations, but Darin continued to come to me for consultation when he found himself facing trying situations.

I am so proud of Darin and his personal and professional changes. He asked if he could meet with our entire leadership team, to seek our understanding and forgiveness. Subsequently, he apologized to, and asked forgiveness of, those individuals he believed he had offended during those early months.

Darin not only went out of his way to be responsive to requests within the organization, he actually went above and beyond. He volunteered for various work groups, attended committee meetings on a regular basis, and became a go-to individual. He initiated and implemented several new support services throughout the hospital. Instead of registering complaints, staff throughout the organization began to compliment him sincerely. The changes have proven to be not only dramatic, but lasting.

At the hospital's Christmas party approximately one year after our private conversation, I was touched when Darin and his wife approached me in a private moment. His wife proceeded to tell me how much she and Darin appreciated the second chance I had provided for Darin—a second chance for a new life—at home and at work.

To this day, I remain touched as I reflect on this near-miss and my privilege to witness such a positive change in someone's life. Please hear me clearly when I emphasize that I am not responsible for these dramatic changes as Darin did this on his own. I only provided an opportunity for him to tell *his story* in a humbling atmosphere without fear of reprisal or demeanor. We all have stories—and we all have personal challenges and shortcomings. Today, I am proud to call Darin "my friend."

4) **Happiness versus Joy**

I believe we all have an inherent need to be happy. I also believe God wants each of us to experience happiness in both our personal and professional lives. For those who believe in God and ascribe to the principles we have discussed, finding and experiencing joy in all things is our ultimate desire—and reward.

For many years of my life, I had used *happiness* and *joy* interchangeably when speaking and writing. In more recent years, I have come to appreciate what I believe distinguishes these two words.

I believe happiness tends to be a temporary human condition, dependent upon *happenings*. Therefore, happiness is often fleeting and temporary in nature, which often finds us looking for the next thing, the next fix. This means we are often left feeling unfulfilled.

If we are solely dependent on achieving happiness, it stands to reason we may experience mood changes from time to time, be inconsistent in temperament, and often unpredictable in our behaviors and interactions with others. You recognize the profile—the individual who is often described as "moody, unpredictable, inconsistent, pessimistic," for example.

By contrast, I believe *joy* comes from a personal relationship with the Lord. Because such a relationship is always present and everlasting, experiencing *joy* is thereby unwavering, ongoing, and lasting. What a wonderful gift for those who experience *joy*. You will recognize this profile as well—the individual who is described as "always being the same, outgoing, cheerful, open-minded, optimistic," for example. These are the individuals we tend to enjoy knowing, working with, and having employed in our organizations. I appreciate these individuals and am always grateful to have them as employees.

I believe God wants us to experience both happiness and joy in our lives. I also believe we can achieve happiness without joy, but not joy without happiness. God does provide us with freedom of choice.

I would be remiss if I did not credit and honor my high school sweetheart, and first wife, for these insights I've come to appreciate. I'll introduce you to Nancy early, as I will reference her at other times throughout the book. She was my best friend here on earth for over forty-four years before she succumbed to an unexpected, massive myocardial infarction.

Nancy was a devoted mother of our two sons and the loving wife to her husband, who respected and loved her immeasurably. Nancy is responsible for many things that have contributed to who I am today. For example, Nancy was the impetus for me to go to college, rather than remain on the farm.

Nancy was a woman of faith. She was the one who helped me appreciate the differences between happiness and joy and challenged me to wear both as an interwoven fabric impregnated with a spirit of optimism in all things. Her quiet, gentle, and confident manner was most effective in encouraging me when I was facing challenging issues. During such conversations, she would say, "Remember, if we all sat down in one large circle, with our shoes representing our individual problems, and we were asked to throw our shoes into the circle; in a short time, we would all be scrambling for our own shoes." She was reminding me, and still is to this day, to be as happy, joyful, and optimistic as possible in all situations, regardless of the circumstances—on and off of the field.

As leaders, we not only have the privilege of modeling specific desired behaviors, we have an obligation to do so. Everything we do has to be genuine in nature and consistent to the point that staff will be able to accurately predict how we will handle specific situations and circumstances.

Other staff, and leaders specifically, will generally follow suit in replicating and modeling the behaviors of the CEO and leadership team. All of these behaviors become foundational blocks in building a culture of truthfulness, transparency, and ownership throughout the organization.

5) Ascribe to Servant Leadership—Mean It and Live It

For most of my years as a hospital CEO, I have openly subscribed to and promoted *servant leadership*. It is not only important to know what servant leadership is; it is important to understand its origination and, perhaps most importantly, to be skilled in recognizing and emulating servant leadership in all aspects of our lives.

With respect to modern-day use of the term, one must credit Mr. Robert K. Greenleaf for coining the term in *The Servant as Leader,* an essay he first published in 1970. With all due respect to Mr. Greenleaf and the work he devoted to its meaning and usage, I prefer to take the concept of servant leadership from Jesus, who came to earth to serve and not to be served. For me, this adds more meaning to this timeless concept.

In the generic use of the word *leader*, we often say (including me), "Everyone can be a leader, on and off the field." Being a servant leader in this context certainly broadens its meaning, credibility, and application to this everyday occupation we call life or living. In its simplest form, servant leadership is really about how we serve and treat one another on a daily basis.

There are many ways we can model servant leadership within the organization and beyond, in our personal lives. When I was out and about within the facility, I made a point of watching for these subtle opportunities. It may be carrying out the trash for someone from environmental services or pushing the patient meal cart to or from the nursing units or answering telephones or call lights when staff are particularly busy. It may be clearing the table by picking up food trays after a staff luncheon meeting or civic organization luncheon.

It is also important to develop a keen eye for others doing little things outside the normal and to acknowledge and affirm their actions as going above and beyond. It is fun to observe how contagious these little gestures become within the organization. When completed with a sense of humbleness, an even stronger message is conveyed to others.

6) **Your Work as a Calling, a Ministry**

Over twenty years ago, I attended the American College of Healthcare Executives (ACHE) Conference in Chicago. A luncheon highlight during the conference was the introduction of the *Hospital CEO of the Year Award,* presented annually to an individual who demonstrated outstanding leadership and organizational talents and accomplishments. There were over 3,000 people at this luncheon. As was customary, the selected individual was asked to share remarks, following the announcement and award presentation.

I do not recall his name or the organization he represented. I have only retained a profile picture of this individual as a tall, muscular, well-dressed gentleman in his late-fifties or early sixties, who wore glasses.

I will always remember, however, how humble he was in his remarks, how he connected with the audience, and these words: "For everyone working in healthcare, I encourage each of you to view your work as a calling, as a ministry and not just a vocation." He went on to say, "This would be my wish and desire for everyone, not just those representing healthcare." I cannot estimate how many times I have relayed this portion of his story. When presented with the opportunity, I share this with others, as I believe it connotes a higher level of purpose and meaning to our chosen work and our lives, both person-ally and professionally.

7) **Ready and Available to Pray**

I believe there is an old adage that goes something like this: *If everything else fails, pray.* I suggest, with rearrangement of words, a better way of saying this may be: *Pray before every-thing else fails.* Even though I strongly believe in the power of prayer, I must admit I do not always keep prayer in its proper place and priority.

I have spoken of seeking God's wisdom in all things. Prayer is the vehicle through which we make these connections and express petitions in seeking His wisdom.

We often express to others that we will keep them (and their family members) in our thoughts and prayers. And then there are times when we ask individuals if there is anything we can do for them during periods of trial and tribulation, and they will respond by saying, "Please pray for me" or "You can pray for me." I have come to believe we should treat this as an invitation to pray right then and there, if circumstances allow; though this should still require their approval to do so.

I have found myself praying with staff members at work in hallways, in their departments, in the parking lot, and in my office. Likewise, I have prayed with patients in their hospital rooms. Praying over the telephone should never be overlooked as an opportunity.

I always make sure individuals grant approval, are com-fortable in doing so, and are not feeling duress in participating in prayer. Many have not only thanked me profusely at the time but have also followed up with texts or personal notes expressing their appreciation for praying with them.

It is interesting that prayer is something we can always do for others and/or for the needs and initiatives they represent. We do not even need the person's approval. Also, I believe it is important to not only pray in times of need but also in times of rejoicing or returning thanks.

There is another personal insight I have come to be attentive to in my life. Have you experienced a time when you have thought of someone on a frequent and reoccurring basis? When this happens to me, I remind myself to be in prayer for them, even without knowing any specific needs they may be experiencing at the time.

I want to introduce you to Mr. McCaslin (Mac), one of my favorite teachers in high school. In addition to my first wife, Nancy, Mr. McCaslin was the second person I credit for my going on to college following graduation. He did not demand my respect, he commanded it. Looking back on it now, Mr. McCaslin was a servant leader.

We both moved out of state some time ago, so we did not visit on a regular basis. Several years ago, I found myself thinking about Mac frequently. I remembered recalling that I should telephone him and tell him one more time how much I respected him and appreciated everything he had done for me.

I found myself putting this off for various reasons over a three-week period. Finally, one evening I called his home in Ohio. His wife, Barb, answered the telephone. After some small talk, I asked if I could speak with Mac. There was this pregnant pause on the other end, after which, Barb said, "Mac died suddenly, approximately two weeks ago."

I was devastated I had not called when I had first started thinking about him. I had missed an opportunity to honor him one more time. Since that time, I have tried to be more mindful to be in prayer when this happens and, perhaps, even contact the individual at my earliest convenience. I will reference Mr. McCaslin again, later in the book, for another purpose. In doing so, I will have done the next best thing, having honored him posthumously.

All of these opportunities also exist in the workplace. As leaders, I believe it is humbling for us to demonstrate (and for staff to witness) that we draw our strength from a much higher power, rather than just relying on our own inner strengths—which again are God-given. Humbleness is an ingredient for an inspiring culture.

Several months ago, a pastor friend of mine texted me early in the morning stating, "God has been prompting me in thinking about you and praying for you. I wanted to make sure you are okay. I have been holding you in prayer and will continue to do so."

At the time, I was not aware of any concerns. I felt fine physically and, to my knowledge, my family members were all okay. It suddenly occurred to me that maybe I was being protected or spared from something. I called him when I arrived at the office and told him how much I appreciated his concern and prayers.

Inspiration Versus Motivation

8) **Introducing and Honoring Renowned Author, Speaker, and Friend**

It is a blessing and privilege to introduce Lance Secretan, PhD, an internationally renowned author, speaker, and personal friend. Many of you are already familiar with Lance and his many fine literary works.

I am humbled to say, throughout my fifty-plus years in progressive leadership roles, Lance Secretan's work has impacted me more, personally and professionally, than all of the many other leadership principles and programs combined. He has been, and continues to be, a special blessing in my life.

Lance has authored over twenty books. His last two books are must-reads. The first is *The Spark, The Flame, and the Torch . . . Inspire Self. Inspire Others. Inspire the World.* This book was published in June, 2010. His last book, *The Bellwether Effect . . . Stop Following. Start Inspiring!* was published and released in May, 2018. I was humbled and blessed to be asked to write the *Foreword* for *The Bellwether Effect.*

In order to provide context to this section, "Inspiration versus Motivation," to honor Lance's fine work, and to describe how I came to know Lance, I am taking the liberty (with his permission) to share portions of the *Foreword,* as follows:

It was fortuitous that I attended the Nebraska Hospital Association Annual Convention in Lincoln, Nebraska. I was also scheduled to attend the Missouri Hospital Association Annual Convention just a couple of weeks later. Given the usual busyness of the fall season and several other commitments during this same period, I reflected on the wisdom of being out of the office for both of these conventions. Even though I was looking forward to attending both, I was particularly drawn to the Nebraska Convention. As it turned out, my intuition was perfectly accurate.

As one of nearly a thousand audience members for the first keynote address of the convention, presented by Lance Secretan, I found myself "hanging on" to every word he said—I had never before seen an audience so captivated. Secretan's focus was on the differences between motivation and inspiration.

The speaker's work and message confirmed my own accumulated beliefs and convictions—and I asked myself, "Why have I not been more assertive and deliberate in a more loving and inspiring manner?" Why had I missed so many opportunities during my career to make personal and professional lives more enjoyable for so many—and encourage them to dream more, personally and on behalf of the organizations I have been called to serve?

A short time later, I participated in the Higher Ground Leadership Retreat at the Secretan Center in Ontario, Canada, personally hosted by Secretan, and soon after, two other members of our leadership team signed up for the retreat as well. A few months later, all seven of our leadership team members had shared this same experience under Dr. Secretan's personal tutelage.

As a result, we are transforming our organization through the application of Higher Ground Leadership and implementing the innovative concepts put forward in *The Bellwether Effect*. This is a remarkable piece of literary work that advances the merits and power of "inspiration" versus "motivation" and "dreams" versus "mission statements." Secretan teaches that "motivation" consists of a combination of two pressure points: fear and material rewards (or punishments). Motivation is seldom about the other person, but more often about me . . . Motivation is largely an attempt to alter or control the behavior of others, raise performance standards, change attitudes or beliefs, or exploit capacity. When we come from this position, we are working principally on the social self, tapping into and exploring the fears of the person we are trying to motivate, relying on shaming, bribing, rewarding, threatening, or pressuring—all of which trigger the primal fear instincts. Secretan helps the reader understand how corporate America has come to develop and practice these behaviors and why we need to change from what I now see as archaic behaviors.

In contrasting motivation, Dr. Secretan reminds us that "Inspiration is intrinsic. Unlike motivation, it does not come from fear, but from love. It is not about me—it is almost exclusively about you. Great leaders and coaches want to inspire others to grow, to accomplish their objectives, to shine, to reach their potential and splendor. Any rewards for these inspiring coaches and leaders come from the joy they experience when helping others to reach their own goals or become larger as fully realized human beings. Therefore, inspiration is an act of love and service to others, whereas motivation is self-centered . . . inspiration is aimed at the essential self—the soul of another, and is most often generated from within—the inspirer is merely the facilitator of the inspired."

I take strength in knowing that inspiration is genuine, lasting, and originates deeply from within each of us and is not just a temporal, topical solution found in many of the tactical, so-called motivational maneuvers we have inflicted on staff and organizations over time. None of these were designed for distance or duration—they are generally just a "flash in the pan."

Lance Secretan has provided a license for me, and so many others, to do the right thing, regardless of what some corporate voices (or Bellwethers) may advocate. He reminds us that "the employee is now the new customer" and that "leadership is about inspiring people, and people—every one of us—are inspired by dreams." I am also struck by his statement, "Over the last fifty years in corporate life, we have expanded our capacity to quantify, measure, and analyze, but we have stifled our capacity to dream." Equally powerful is, "A mission statement may be about you, but a dream is about serving others and how you will serve them."

Of all of the riveting statements in The Bellwether Effect, this is my favorite: "Motivation is lighting a fire under someone; inspiration is lighting a fire within someone."

This book is bound to light a fire within all who read it and apply its message to ignite positive differences in their lives and organizations—and thus in our world.

I strongly encourage you to read both of Lance's most recent books. I believe *The Spark, the Flame, and the Torch . . . Inspire Self. Inspire Others. Inspire the World* is a precursor to *The Bellwether Effect* and will be instrumental in further embellishing the wisdom and insight found in *The Bellwether Effect*.

I would never pretend I could add anything to Lance's phenomenal work regarding inspiration versus motivation. At the same time, I want to emphasize that I am definitely a student of Lance Secretan and cannot adequately express my admiration for his work.

The overall purpose of my book is to provide practical recommendations in establishing and maintaining an inspiring, loving, servant leader culture.

I am also writing to prospective employees, encouraging them (you) to search out organizations that either demonstrate an inspiring, loving, servant leader culture or are transparent in defining plans to achieve such a culture.

Within the first thirty to forty-five minutes after walking into an organization, you will be able to sense whether or not such a culture exists within its walls. I cannot estimate how many times I have heard comments from individuals visiting our organization(s) for the first time. Paraphrasing, the comments could be summarized to the effect, "There is just something different here. I sensed it when I walked-in." The list would include job candidates, vendors, representatives from other healthcare facilities, community organizations, surveyors, patients, family members; and yes, patient visitors. If you are insistent in finding such an organization, you will have also contributed to what Lance refers to as "changing the world."

In the first section of the book entitled, "Spiritual Beliefs and Underpinnings," I shared principles that are important to me as an individual, a husband, a father, an employee, a CEO, and a citizen of this great country. If I am going to be successful in inspiring others, I must first be inspired myself. I draw my strength and inspiration from my Lord, Jesus Christ.

In the following sections, I will share principles I have found helpful to this end. You may choose to make these your own, which will strengthen your personal convictions as a seasoned leader, an aspiring leader, or a job candidate wanting to find a difference—and make a difference.

9) Inspiration Universal

Generally, when we speak of *culture,* our minds immediately go to the workplace. Even though we usually do not describe our home environments as being a culture, I contend everything does and should start at home. How often have we heard, "It all starts at home"?

It is in our home environments where we are first exposed to the attitudes and behaviors that make us who we are throughout life. Home is where most of us first learn to love, to share, to encourage and to be encouraged, to learn, to mentor, to be patient, to assume responsibility, to work as a team, and yes, to be inspired and to inspire others. It is interesting these attributes mirror those we yearn for in our workplaces, but seldom fully experience.

I particularly like what Lance Secretan said in the *The Bellwether Effect:* "There is just one thing we need to teach leaders who wish to be great and to inspire others, and that is how to love, and it is surprising how many are still afraid to do so. Love is not about maximizing what we can get; it is about maximizing what we can give."

For something so inherently needed and appreciated, as humans, why have we drifted away and allowed ourselves to become complacent in playing by two separate and opposing sets of rules—one for home and the other for work.

It should not be surprising that many individuals have not mastered the switching off between home and work successfully, which only adds to this dichotomy and, ultimately, places unnecessary stress on both the work unit and the family unit. It is much easier to play by just one set of rules.

Several years ago, I worked with Joe, a colleague who found great satisfaction in having everyone around him know how successful he was in separating his home and work lives. Joe would further explain that there was a stop sign approximately midway between his home and his place of work. As Joe stopped at the stop sign on his way home from work, he would visualize opening his car door and setting his briefcase by the stop sign and driving off towards home, totally oblivious of anything that had happened at work.

The next day, as he stopped by the stop sign on his way to work, he would visualize picking up his briefcase and proceeding to work, totally oblivious of anything that had happened at home.

I have never been able to separate these two environments as effectively as Joe described. If I were to visit with him about this, I would challenge him with this admonishment: It may have been more like you're setting the "*Work* Playbook" by the sign and picking up the "*Home* Playbook," on his way home—and vice versa the next morning.

I was blessed to have grown up in a very loving home, even though I do not remember my parents ever telling me they loved me. I believe my parents had grown up in a home and culture where doing so was not practiced; and perhaps, even considered a sign of personal weakness.

It is interesting I never questioned whether or not I was loved—I just knew. It begs the question, "How did I know I was loved if I was never told by my parents?" I knew because of the way they always cared for me; provided a safe and encouraging environment; wanted the best things for me; respected my feelings; challenged me with responsibility; taught me right from wrong; and yes, taught me how to work. They inspired me to be the best I can be.

Contrary to, and because of our upbringing, Nancy and I as parents of two sons would never part for the day or end the day, without telling them how much we loved them. In actuality we, as family members, would tell one another several times a day. Even now, as adult men and as a family separated by distance, this still holds true. We predictably end our conversations, verbally or in writing, by saying "I love you" to one another. I am confident our sons would be quick to say they grew up in a loving home. Certainly, just saying "I love you" did not make it so, but it certainly was and is an affirmation of the characteristics described previously, "It all starts at home."

In the first portion of this segment, I identified several attributes families strive to practice in providing nurturing, loving, and inspiring homes and reflected relationships with those they care about unconditionally. These attributes are important to us in our family lives, yet we do not exhibit the same tenacity for replicating and establishing these characteristic relationships at work. Whether at home or at work, we are the same individuals with the same attributes, the same needs, the same desires, the same dreams, and the same responses to an inspiring environment. Why is this? Sadly, most of us spend more time with others at work, than we do with our own families.

It is not that we lack desire for such work environments. Over a period of many years, we have progressively become conditioned to and accepting of the fact that the work environment will be different from our family life.

Throughout the remaining portions of this book, I will share practical suggestions and recommendations, specifically for the seasoned leader; the aspiring leader; and the individual seeking employment *with* inspiring organizations.

During my fifty-plus years, no one has ever worked *for* me; an innumerable number of individuals have worked *with* me. Symbolically, if all three of the above individuals were employed with the same organization, my goal would be that they work collaboratively to create and maintain an inspiring and loving work environment (culture) for all employed there—and all those conducting business with the organization. Assuredly, it will not only make *good sense*, but also, *good cents.*

Humanity and good business call for *setting fires within* individuals, not *under them*, or as Lance would remind us, "Inspiration is setting a fire within someone; Motivation is setting a fire under someone." The only time we should be capable of motivating anyone, is when loss of life or limb is threatened and we need to motivate individuals to move away from the danger quickly and effectively.

Inspiration and *motivation* are often used interchangeably to mean the same thing. As we have come to understand, the two could not be further apart in meaning and practice. I suggest we take every opportunity to model and help others understand the difference—and to create *inspirational* cultures at the expense of *motivational* cultures.

10) Never Break the Spirit

Growing up on the farm, I spent a great deal of time with my paternal grandmother and grandfather. I have always appreciated the extra time they devoted to me while my parents were working hard to eke out a living for a family of six. As the oldest of two brothers and two sisters, I was able to command most of my grandparents' attention for a number of years.

One of my fondest memories with my grandfather, Charlie, centers on his last team of horses, King and Queen. My grandfather had farmed with big, heavy workhorses for many of his active years as a farmer in Nebraska. As tractors replaced horses for the heavy work on the farm, the workhorses became relegated to light farm work, or in some cases, hobby farming.

I was seven or eight years old, when I recall sitting between my grandfather's legs as we raked alfalfa hay with King and Queen. I remember how big and massive these two bay-colored Belgians appeared, as they pulled forward together in perfect timing and coordination to the right, to the left, and back again. Even though, they were guided by the reins he held, I remember how they responded to his verbal commands. I will never forget how thrilled I was to hold the reins, believing I had total control of these two perfectly matched hulks. Little did I realize; the horses were merely responding to my grandfather's verbal call-outs.

My grandfather and I would have several conversations about his respect for the many saddle horses and workhorses that had contributed to his family's livelihood for so many years of his life. I had inherited a special interest in horses and considered myself a cowboy in those formative years.

My grandfather, "Gramp," and I would often visit about his experiences in training and caring for horses. He would emphasize that respect for the horse was of utmost importance. He would tell me how important it was to train and manage horses through a sense of expectation and specific performance. Then he would quickly follow with, "You need to let the horse know what you expect, but never, never break the horse's spirit." This comment has always stayed with me and has come to mean more to me as the years have passed.

I will never forget when Gramp made his final decision to sell his favored King and Queen. There was little need for the horses any longer on the farm, as tractors and other equipment(s) had totally revolutionized farming practices. Likewise, I will never forget the day the new owners arrived with their truck to haul King and Queen away to their new home.

I only remember seeing my Gramp cry two times. As the loaded truck drove away from our farm that day, I looked up into my grandfather's face to see tears streaming down his face. As a stoic man, he attempted to hide his emotions. At that moment, I more fully understood how much he loved and respected those two horses. I also came to admire and remember, after all of these years, the significance of "training and handling horses with expectation, but never breaking the spirit." The only other time I saw Gramp cry was when my grandmother, his lifelong best friend and companion, died several years later.

As leaders, it is our responsibility to assure staff are properly trained, oriented, and supported by communicating a sense of expectation on behalf of the organization. This is important; however, it is even more important that we not "break the individual's spirit" in doing so.

The dictionary defines *spirit* as "the non-physical part of a person which is the seat of emotions and character, the soul, the prevailing or typical mood." How can we expect top individual, or collective, performance when we demoralize or break the spirits of those we are dependent on for making our organizations successful? This often occurs when we exercise certain techniques under the guise of motivational approaches, which result in "lighting a fire under someone."

The dictionary tells us *inspire* means "to excite, encourage, or breathe life into." *Inspire* comes from the Latin word that means to inflame or to blow into. When you inspire something, it is as if you are blowing air over a low flame to make it grow . . . "fill (someone) with the urge or ability to do or feel something, especially to do something creative."

An additional insight: "To inspire from the Latin *spirare*, meaning 'spirit' to affect, guide, or arouse by divine influence; to fill with enlivening or exalting emotion, to animate; a divine influence upon human beings, to give life, the breath of God."

To illustrate the contrast, it would be more appropriate to speak of *dis-inspiring* (breaking the spirit of someone), compared to *inspiring* someone. I deeply regret the times I may have inadvertently and inappropriately *dis-inspired* someone during the early portion of my career. I do, however, take relish in memories of those who have credited me for inspiring them positively in their personal and/or professional lives.

Takeaways:

Leaders:

1) Avoid using the terms *motivation* and *inspiration* interchangeably to mean the same thing. Understand the difference and take every opportunity to make and verbalize the distinction.

2) On opposite ends of the spectrum you will find *dis-inspiring* and *inspiring*. Both are powerful, the first in a negative sense and the second, in a positive manner. Come to believe, experience, and appreciate this difference and the powerful effects an inspirational culture will have on staff and your organization.

3) Take every opportunity to model these positive and powerful behaviors. Actions do speak louder than words.

Employees:

1) When applying for a new position with a new organization, look for clues and ask questions that will help you determine whether or not the organization embraces an inspiring, loving, servant leader culture.

2) Examine yourself. Are you an inspirational and loving person; if not, consider learning more and committing to becoming a difference-maker in your current organization or the new organization you plan to join. Remember, we can all be leaders. Adopt a personal policy to *bloom and produce fruit wherever you are planted.*

11) Teach and Learn How to Work

I have been working for as long as I can remember, beginning as a lad growing up on our family farm, but this may be a bit of an exaggeration with threads of truthfulness. Perhaps, a better way of expressing this is to say, "I have assumed various levels of responsibility for as long as I can remember." For example, my dad would give me the little runt and orphaned piglets to feed and care for as my very own. Caring for other living things taught me a great deal about some of life's basic principles.

Outside of school, school activities, and study time, I spent almost every possible minute with my dad. Farmer neighbors would often describe me as my dad's shadow. We worked together on the farm until I left for college as a freshman and after that for three summers until marriage and graduation. Having lost my dad at the young age of fifty-six years, I am so thankful we had all of these early years together.

I respected and admired my dad very much. I learned a great deal from him, mostly about life in general. Both of us graduated eighth grade from the same one-room country school. This is where our educational similarities ended. When he graduated from the eighth grade, his dad (my grandfather) expected him to forgo a high school education and work on the farm.

I am so proud of what my dad was able to accomplish in spite of his limited education. He would go on to establish a successful farming and cattle operation. He would be elected to the local School Board for consecutive terms, would serve for several terms in the elected position of County Supervisor, and would serve on the board of directors of a prominent midwestern agricultural lending institution.

Dad would tell me there were many things he would not be able to teach me because of his limited eighth grade education; however, he was going to teach me *how to work*. At the time, this sounded so trite. My typical response was, "Dad, what do you mean, we work together all of the time?" He would go on to say, "If I teach you how to work, you will always be able to take care of your family."

As the years have passed, these comments have meant a great deal to me. I have come to appreciate what he was actually saying to me, in my words and not his. I believe he was describing the importance of giving a good day's work for a day's pay; being reliable by reporting promptly for work and staying as long as agreed (or needed); being a person of integrity with truthfulness in all matters; having a good attitude and being respectful in my interactions with others; assuming responsibility and being accountable for my actions; grasping every opportunity to do a little more than expected; offering creative ideas and suggestions through a sense of ownership; and *propping others up* and *not tearing them down.*

I now know he was inspiring me to be the best I could be, personally and professionally. *Inspiring* or *inspiration* are words that were not in his vocabulary. Even so, he identified these inherent needs in me and others; in turn, he was convicted to fill these voids through inspirational approaches. I know this to be true, because I witnessed these attributes in his many relationships with others.

In my own situation, he inspired me to move from the runt and orphaned piglets to owning a hog operation, a small herd of cattle, a sizable flock of sheep, purchasing my own tractor with a number of tilling attachments, and farming over fifty acres of cornland.

Prior to leaving for college, I liquidated all of these assets. The net proceeds from these sales totaled enough for me to independently pay for my first three semesters of college. My dad realized it was not just about the money, for he knew I would learn a great deal from these responsibilities and experiences. He inspired me to learn how to work, to be able to always care for my family, and to consistently strive to be the best I can be. Even though he only had an eighth-grade education, he was a smart man.

I had been at one of my CEO positions for approximately three months when an interesting situation occurred that I have always remembered. Diane, the accounts payable/payroll manager, had been with the organization in her position for over ten years and was well-respected in a responsible role.

One afternoon, she stepped to my office door and asked if she could visit with me for a few minutes. I always try to be immediately available, so my response was "Yes, certainly—please have a chair." After some small talk, she asked if she could ask me a question. I have long forgotten what the question was, but I will always remember my question back to her and her response.

Regarding what she saw as a challenging dilemma, Diane looked directly into my eyes and asked, "What should I do?" I paused and responded with "What do you believe you should do?" She, in turn, paused for several seconds as though stunned to be asked and then replied, "No one has ever asked me that before." What she was really saying was that, beyond the prescriptive and routine, no one had ever inspired her to be creative, to reason and think on her own, or to assume responsibility for her decisions beyond the routine. Even though this aspect of our conversation was never discussed, I believe this was not only an inspirational moment for me, but definitely for her, as I would come to witness her personal growth within the organization.

Takeaways:

Leaders:

1) Make it a habit to inspire others to be the best they are capable of being. Help them see the possibilities in themselves, that they are not able to see by themselves. Believe this is the best use of your time as a leader.

2) Be a risk-taker and investor in practicing as an inspiring, loving, servant leader, since the personal and professional

rewards are endless. What can be more gratifying than to personally witness others blooming where they are planted? What can be better for business than improving productivity, reducing turnover, and improving the bottom line?

Employees:

1) Learn what an inspired employee and workforce looks like and do everything you can to emulate these behaviors.

2) When searching for a position, frame your interview questions to sense the presence of an inspiring, loving, servant leader culture, if it exists. If you do not sense it, it does not exist, and you should consider moving on to the next opportunity.

3) You deserve to find happiness and joy in your work environment. You should also feel an obligation to make it so for those you work with on a daily basis.

12) Focus on Processes and Systems First

I do not believe there are many individuals in our workforce today who go to work for the sole purpose of making everyone else miserable or intentionally causing harm to the organization.

I do believe there is an astronomical number of individuals who go to work daily for uninspiring organizations that drain happiness, joy, and fulfillment from individual employees. This human condition may contribute to making them miserable to be around and result in lower productivity for the organization; thus, subtly harming the organization individually and collectively.

Predictably, you have witnessed this for yourself in the individual who starts a new job with spirit, vigor, and great ambition, only to gradually wane to just *doing their job*, as they may describe their work environment—providing they have not already left the organization in pursuit of another that will fulfill their inherent needs. Having lost this employee, we have added insult to injury as the productivity has not only suffered, but we now have additional costs related to employee turnover.

There is a myriad of approaches leaders can take to create and sustain inspiring and loving cultures. In this section, I will discuss three principles I believe are basic to building such a culture. *First,* I suggest adopting a mindset that *every employee has an inherent need to be accountable.* You may be thinking I am being grandiose, rather Pollyanna in making such a statement. As leaders, it is our responsibility to create a culture that inspires every employee to feel accountable for their contributions, *regardless of their position or status* within the organization—and to provide the tools they need to be successful.

Second, when we identify operational inefficiencies, we should *always examine our processes and systems first,* rather than automatically accusing the individual(s) as having poor performance. Blatant or malicious behavior may prove to be an exception to this approach, but adopting this mindset will make you a better leader.

I believe 95+ percent of the time, we will find enhancements and solutions in improving our processes, our systems. This is the admirable, humane first step; instead of falsely accusing individuals or work groups for inefficiencies, poor quality, inadequate productivity, and other accusations we often make in the workplace, we can focus on the inanimate properties of our processes and systems.

If managed correctly, a thorough examination of our processes and systems will call for an in-depth analysis centering on numbers, data, and other applicable information. If properly facilitated, doing so will remove emotionality from the considerations; thus, reducing the tendency for finger-pointing or undue criticism. We need to remember numbers do not lie; however, people have been known to lie about numbers.

This approach is more apt to create a spirit of camaraderie and a sense that "We are all in this together."

As managers and organizations, we should be as compassionate as possible with individuals; but absolutely relentless on our processes and systems.

It is also important to involve individuals closest to the work under examination in these work groups. This should not be another group of managers trying to affirm what they do not know to be absolutely true. We should find ways to get every employee involved in some fashion within the organization—and this is one excellent way to do this.

In his acclaimed study, *"The Iceberg of Ignorance,"* Sidney Yoshida concluded the following, which supports this premise:

(1) Only 4 percent of problems are known to top managers. This means 96 percent of problems are _not_ known to top managers.
(2) Only 9 percent of problems are known to middle management.
(3) 74 percent of problems are known to supervisors.
(4) 100 percent of problems are known to frontline employees.

The employees involved in these analyses will take ownership for positive results and feel inspired to have been given the opportunity, latitude, and recognition in effecting changes in the workplace, resulting in desired outcomes. Do not forget to publicly recognize these work groups and find a way to celebrate them and their accomplishments. You will be pleased to witness improvements in productivity, reduced costs associated with less turnover, and a happier, more joyful work environment.

Third, never underestimate what dedicated employees will do in spite of poorly-designed and maintained processes, to serve others. Through process analyses, you may be surprised to learn about the work-arounds employees create in spite of sometimes poorly designed work processes and systems, just to make things work and/or meet the needs of the customer. For example, when facing a thrust to reduce expenditures for basic customer (patients in one example) supplies, employees have been known to provide such items at their personal expense—often unbeknown to the managers or organization. Quite remarkable—and admirable.

13) Becoming What We Think About, Talk About, Dream About, and Profess to Be Important

We become what we think about, talk about, dream about, and profess to be important. For me, this has become a meaningful mantra for the past twelve-plus years because it applies to everything in my life, personally and professionally. I have strong convictions regarding the reality and applicability of this statement. For my purposes, I project the inherent *good* associated with its reality. Ironically, this philosophy can not only move us towards great outcomes, but it can also move others towards evil outcomes.

I had accepted the CEO position with a rural healthcare system for several reasons. The overarching reason for my attraction to the position stemmed from the organization's commitment to construct a new hospital and renovate much of the old facility.

Not only did I endorse the construction project, I recognized the opportunity for significant vertical and horizontal growth within this rural healthcare system. As the central focus, or the hub of the system, the old, outdated hospital facility had become the growth-limiting factor—the weakest link. Many of the other necessary resources to support significant growth already existed within the system.

Previous initiatives to construct a new hospital had failed. In the view of many staff and community members, there was this underlying sentiment of, "We will believe it when we see it. Similar commitments have failed at the eleventh hour before." We believed an important part of our job, as a leadership team, was to stimulate dreaming for the future of the system, centering on the construction of the new facility and growth of new and existing services.

For these reasons, my commitment in taking the job had centered on unequivocal assurances this new construction project would come to fruition. As such, I was totally confident in the board of directors' commitment to the construction of the new hospital.

At the time, we believed there were two choices for making these growth related dreams come true. Both approaches centered on the movie theme from *The Field of Dreams* for different reasons. We believed one of the tendencies we would need to avoid centered on this theme, "Just build it, and they will come."

With the construction of the new hospital, the organization had committed to a significant increase in its short-term and long-term debt load. I and others, took this seriously in making this a significant factor in our dreaming processes. With this in mind, we believed it was our responsibility, as a leadership team, to be the catalyst in making these dreams come true sooner, rather than later.

I will always remember how I could feel the overall change in attitude that turned over when that first shovel of dirt turned over during the groundbreaking ceremony, *"Wow, this is really going to happen, sort of change."* Everyone was so excited—and the race had begun.

Our leadership team had been considering our approach in facilitating this dream through committed inspiring, loving, servant leadership. Back to the two options I had identified.

The first was to do nothing differently during the construction plan, adopting the philosophy, *"Build it, and they will come,"* with hopes for a flood of new business when our new doors opened. We were not convinced the sole attraction of a new, flashy facility would automatically improve our volumes and associated revenues.

The *second* option was to become aggressive in creating new vertical and horizontal growth throughout the system immediately—and then move these new services, programs, and volumes into the new hospital when it opened. This second option was the more appealing. From a financial perspective, this option made the most *sense* and the most *cents*.

Our leadership team believed we needed to create a theme everyone could understand, appreciate, believe in, support, and dream about. It was at this time, we created this mantra, *"We become what we think about, talk about, dream about, and profess to be important."* The timing was perfect. So much of the new construction project was embedded in this mantra, and we witnessed these construction and growth dreams coming true right before our eyes.

We took every opportunity to reinforce this mantra and share our progress, as we moved towards our open house date. The mantra was replicated on everything from our board reports to our verbal and written communications. The enthusiasm, creativity, and support from the staff was phenomenal.

New programs and services were springing up throughout our service area. We were experiencing month over month growth in many of our existing services. As planned, we "moved these successful endeavors into our new facility," when it opened fourteen months later. In actual fact, *"We had become what we thought about, talked about, dreamed about, and had professed as being important."*

Dr. Barton Goldsmith, psychotherapist and author, contributes to our daily newspaper as a columnist on a regular basis. Recently, in his article entitled, "Visualization for Success," he shared these comments:

The lessons are very clear. Our thoughts do create our reality, and we are almost always thinking. If you keep the thoughts positive, more good things happen. You can create a lot of what you want with intention and some internal visioning, and most of the time it's easier than you think. So, what's stopping you?

14) Out with Fear; In with Love and Inspiration

We must be more persistent in replacing fear within our organizations. Lance Secretan speaks of fear as the first of the big eight *demotivators.* In his book, *The Bellwether Effect,* he says, "We are born with love, but we learn fear." He emphasizes, "We must move from fear to love."

In the early 1990s, I was privileged to attend one of the last of Dr. W. Edwards Deming's presentations. In his book, *Out of the Crisis,* published in 1986, this is what Dr. Deming said about fear, as included within his bolded section, **"Drive out fear."**

> No one can put in his best performance unless he feels secure. ***Se* comes from the Latin, meaning "without," *cure* means "fear" or "care." *Secure* means "without fear,"** not afraid to express ideas, not afraid to ask questions. Fear takes on many faces. A common denominator of fear in any form, anywhere, is loss from impaired performance and padded figures. (emphasis added)

I think each of us in a leadership role must honestly ask ourselves, *"How successful have we really been, regarding this endeavor in the last thirty-five to forty years?"* We must press on, as improving the human condition is always a worthy cause. Love and inspiration will naturally occupy and swell within spaces vacated by fear and motivation. I am taking the liberty to modify a lyric from of a song of the past, *"Love rushes in where fear dares not to tread."*

15) The Buck Stops . . . and Starts with the CEO

History tells us President Truman kept a small engraved placard on the corner of his desk that read, *"The Buck Stops Here."* As we examine requirements to establish and maintain an inspirational, loving culture, it is only fitting we identify the CEO as the responsible and accountable individual. I contend, *"The Buck Not Only Stops with the CEO, It Starts with the CEO."* This is one of the responsibilities of a CEO (or such a leader by any other name) that cannot and should not be delegated by the CEO.

Everyone in the organization is ultimately responsible for the culture of an organization. The CEO is responsible for modeling *Inspirational, Loving, Servant Leadership* to the leadership team; The leadership team (which includes the CEO) is responsible for modeling *Inspirational, Loving, Servant Leadership* to the rest of the management team (comprised of department directors, managers, and supervisors); and the management team, in concert with the leadership team, is responsible for modeling *Inspirational, Loving, Servant Leadership* to all staff, throughout the entire organization.

Formal leaders at all levels of government, society, and our organizations should possess and model the characteristics and behaviors of *Inspirational, Loving, Servant Leadership*—those the majority of us desire to emulate and adopt as our own. If this were to occur universally, can you imagine what our families, our organizations, our states, this country, and the world would look like—and what that world might be able to accomplish in the name of humanity?

The development of an inspiring, loving, servant leader culture can be a very contagious movement. Mr. Joe Tye, author of *The Florence Prescription*, contends when a movement reaches 30 percent participation/buy-in, there is no turning back. Joe refers to this as the *tipping point*. I am reminded from sociology *a tipping point is a point in time when a group—or many group members—rapidly and dramatically changes its behavior by widely adopting a previously rare practice.*

In following sections, we will examine everyone's role in establishing and maintaining an inspiring, loving, servant culture.

THE SPARK, THE FLAME, AND THE TORCH … INSPIRE SELF. INSPIRE OTHERS. INSPIRE THE WORLD.

I have chosen to identify what I believe are the necessary attributes, characteristics, and behaviors of each of the above sections through an application of Lance Secretan's book, *The Spark, the Flame, and the Torch . . . Inspire Self. Inspire Others. Inspire the World.*

As a reminder, my intended reader audience includes, (1) CEOs, (2) leadership team members, (3) management staff, (4) individuals who are aspiring to leadership roles at all levels, (5) existing staff who want to contribute to a more inspirational, loving culture, and (6) individuals who are seeking employment in high performing, inspirational organizations.

Roll-Out Plan
Everything in this book applies to all individuals who desire to enrich their lives and the lives of those around them.

The purpose of this roll-out plan is to provide a summary road map for the rest of this book.

Conceptually, as a visual individual, I suggest you imagine a large snowball (starting with the Foreword and proceeding sections) rolling down the hill through "The Spark," "The Flame," and "The Torch" sections. As it rolls through each section of the book, it becomes larger and larger with all the accumulating information being carried along to add meaning and understanding to each subsequent section, until it comes to rest at the bottom of the hill—the end of the book. The snowball, being circular in structure, builds on itself as it tumbles downhill; and the slope of the hill is linear in structure, symbolizing maturation and distribution of influence as the snowball picks up speed and momentum.

Everything discussed to this point, builds-on and rolls over into "The Spark" section; everything in "The Spark" section builds-on and rolls over into "The Flame" section; and everything in "The Flame" section builds-on and rolls over into "The Torch" section.

As you contemplate building an inspiring organization, undergirded with inspiring, loving, servant leadership, I offer a second visual: Please visualize the requirements in building a new house, fully-adorned with beautiful landscaping to be shared with your new neighbors, in your new neighborhood.

The basic requirements of building a house, to be completed with expertise, are those listed below. Parallels can be drawn to the requirements of building an inspiring culture and organization, based on a strong foundation of inspiring, loving, servant leadership:

Requirements for Building a New House and Requirements for Building an Inspiring Organization

1) Land on which to build—*Commitment to Create Inspiring, Loving, Servant Leadership*
2) Solid foundation—***The Spark*** *. . . Personal Commitment to Inspiring, Loving Attributes*

3) Walls, roof, exterior—***The Flame*** . . . *Inspiring Others to Join in Construction*

4) Beautiful landscaping (water features, rocks, trees, shrubs, flowers)—***The Torch*** . . . *Inspiring Beyond Work (Sharing the beauty of your new home, with new neighbors, in your new neighborhood)*

Rolling Along: Through Detailed Review

IGNITING THE SPARK...
INSPIRE SELF

This chapter includes twenty-eight practical suggestions and recommendations to inspire self (you) in preparation for what lies beyond—to inspire others.

For discussion purposes, primary focus in this section is on the CEO, even though the following are universal and unlimited in nature, applying to each of us. After all, *"The Buck Starts and Stops with the CEO,"* regardless if he/she is currently a CEO in an uninspiring organization, new to an uninspiring organization, or new to an existing inspiring, loving organization.

I contend these will be helpful to the individual who (1) is or becomes a believer in the benefits associated with inspiring, loving, servant leader cultures, (2) lives each day with such conviction, (3) converts these to habits for everyday living, (4) effectively models inspirational, loving, servant leadership at home and at work, and (5) is willing to personally invest in staff at all levels.

1) **Pebble Theory**

One of my fondest memories with my paternal grandparents, Hannah and Charles, was when I was seven years old and they would take me fishing. We would fish in our farm ponds, which provided flood control and water for our cattle herd. These ponds were glassy-smooth on most days.

I enjoyed fishing and spending the time with my grandparents, but if the fish did not start biting within the first fifteen minutes after wetting our lines, I would become bored and turn to other activities, such as throwing pebbles into the water. I remember first the splash and then the concentric rings, emanating outward from the point of entry—endlessly in all directions. To this day, I recall this vividly.

I recommend you subscribe to the theory of a pebble thrown into a smooth pond and the emanating concentric ripples that are generated. Be the pebble that creates life-changing ripples in the lives of others and accept the fact you may never know the full extent of the ripples generated—the ripples representing the differences made in the individual, their family, work, church, community organizations, and perhaps, their address for eternity. You may never know, but they will never forget.

2) God's Purpose for Two Ears and One Mouth

Make your conversations sincerely about others, rather than about yourself. If they tire from talking about themselves, they will change the subject. This demonstrates interest in others, often puts the other person at ease, and is a courtesy often overlooked.

Doing this must be coupled with good listening skills and humbleness. Develop good listening skills so when you finally do speak, everyone will know you were not just hearing but truly listening in an empathetic manner. If not, the intended gracious consideration may be replaced with an impression of insincerity and a lack of interest, and you will have lost opportunity to build a new relationship or enhance an existing one.

It has been said, *Love is the first step to effective listening.* Perhaps, this applies to all types of love. For our purposes, as we speak of inspiring, loving, servant leadership, I believe we are aligning most closely with *agape* love. Paul tells us in 1 Corinthians, "Love is patient, love is kind, it does not envy, it does not boast, it is not proud" (1 Cor. 13:4 NIV).

Each of these four words, *inspiring, loving, servant leadership* are powerful as they stand alone; however, when they're strung together, they describe a formidable strength of character we desire and seek in a leader:

> ***Inspiring:*** lighting a fire within someone;
> ***Loving:*** patient, kind, does not envy, does not boast, is not proud;
> ***Servant:*** one who comes to serve and not be served; and
> ***Leadership:*** the position or function of a leader, a person who guides or directs a group.

It should become very clear why *love is the first step to good listening.* Great leaders are great listeners.

If these are attributes each of us desire in a leader, and leaders have the same need (as everyone is accountable to another leader or group of leaders), why do we continue to witness example after example of the antithesis of the above? Perhaps, we are not as good at loving as some of us pretend to be.

One must conclude that good listening skills are vital in becoming an inspiring, loving, servant leader.

3) Make Bigger Those Who Feel Small and the Big, No Bigger Than They Are

Go out of your way to make bigger those who are made to feel small and the big, no bigger than they are. This is not intended as a demeaning remark; nor am I suggesting one position is more important than another—and I certainly am not referring to physical stature.

First, speak often in a reassuring manner that every position within the organization is important, emphasize that we all play different positions and, just like an athletic team, we are all on *one* team, playing different, but necessary, positions.

Second, individuals working in lower-paid positions often view themselves as being less important—or are made to feel less important by others. We need to guard against this happening in our organizations, because it is absolutely wrong and should not be tolerated. And, it is not inspiring or loving.

Third, make a point of getting to know *everyone* in the organization as well as is logistically possible, depending on the size of the organization. *Everyone* includes every individual, especially those working in food services, housekeeping, maintenance, and other "support" roles.

I am not suggesting you patronize these individuals at the expense of others; however, I do recommend taking a special interest in meeting them where they are, addressing them by their first name, expressing appreciation for their contributions, emphasizing the importance of their work to the organization, encouraging them to become involved in work groups, and seeking their opinions on particular issues.

It is important to approach all of these scenarios as sincerely and consistently as possible; otherwise, your actions may be interpreted negatively, falling short of the intended purposes. It is also important to model such interest in the presence of others, being careful not to demonstrate deference in how you interact with those in more prominent positions.

Referring to someone by their first name, is truly music to their ears. If you were not born with a special gift of remembering names, hone this skill and recognize this as a talent or behavior to be learned. How often have you heard someone say, *"I am just not good at remembering names"*—and they are not, as they share the same excuse time after time? I suggest in an organization of up to approximately 200 employees, it is not unreasonable to expect yourself to remember at least the first name of each employee.

It is also important to not only develop an interest in the individual employee, but also in their family members, as far as you are able to do so. It is helpful to identify and remember one or two things about each employee that you can create casual conversation around from time to time. Employees will be grateful for your sincere interest and thoughtfulness. I refer to this leadership orientation as being employee-centered and family-focused.

As I have left each organization, I have been humbled and inspired to have individuals from the above departments express both publicly and privately how much they appreciated that I always treated them with respect and dignity, remembered their first name, and demonstrated a sincere interest in their work and contributions to the organization. They would tell me I had made them feel important. I have been gratified with similar comments from others, and these are the ones I have come to remember and most cherish during my career.

4)   Your Word as Your Bond

Become known for your word being your bond and that everyone can come to count on it and on you. As an officer of the organization, you will have many opportunities to hone this attribute, but perhaps only one or two to become known for your word *not* being your bond. I am reminded of the adage, *We all have just one opportunity to make a good first impression. In her book Letting Go of Mr. Wrong,* Sonya Parker embellishes this with, "Almost everyone will make a good first impression, but only a few will make a good lasting impression."

This pertains to everything you do and say, ranging from commitments made to the board of directors, customers, staff members, vendors, community organizations, and the public in general. Many of your commitments will be cemented with written contracts and agreements. Most of the interactions I am referring to will be verbal in nature.

If you need to go back on your word, I recommend taking total responsibility as soon as possible; communicating verbally face-to-face; being truthful; apologizing; providing reasons for the retraction, if appropriate; avoid blaming others; and be humble and sincere in your messaging.

An interesting phenomenon often occurs. The manner in which you handle the retraction may transform a perceived weakness into an acknowledged strength on your behalf and that of the organization.

As the CEO, it is also important to remember the line between the CEO and the organization is blurred. In other words, when the public sees you, they see the organization and vice versa. It is also prudent to be mindful that, as an officer, you are representing the board of directors who have collective and individual fiduciary responsibility for the organization.

5) Speaking and Writing, Two of the Same

Often, when considering our writing and speaking skills, we believe we are better at one or the other, and perhaps this is true for some. For consistency purposes, it is important to strive to make these two God-given gifts as congruent as possible. Doing so, reduces discrepancies between what you say and what you write; particularly, when you write about what you said.

Right or wrong, we are judged by others on the basis of how we write and speak. Once again, we only have one opportunity to make a good first impression. I have found the following skills are important to mirror in my personal and professional lives. These skills can be developed and honed intentionally and deliberately.

First, I emphasize being relentless in writing with accurate spelling, grammar, and sentence structure. This applies to *everything* we write, beginning with our text messages, email messages, and hand-written notes. It is also important to proofread *everything* you write—yes, text and email messages included. Given the potential extensive distribution with a flick of our finger or that of others, it is even more important to take extra time to proofread our messages.

I am reminded of Dan, the department director, who innocently responded to an all-staff email without proofreading prior to hitting the send button. Unknowingly to him, his response added a sexually oriented twist to a serious operational, all-staff email. After receiving several telephone calls, he was quick to apologize and make the correction. Everyone had a good laugh at Dan's expense. He was embarrassed and humiliated. This was not his intention, but mistakes like this (along with misspellings, poor grammar, and incomplete sentences) can leave the reader questioning the author's attention to detail in other facets of his/her life, such as work. As a director, responsible for a detailed-oriented healthcare department, such impressions may tarnish his other commendable traits unfairly.

Second, develop a knack for speaking and writing in a tactful, diplomatic fashion regardless of the formality or informality of the topic. Such writing will reinforce the quality of your speaking and such speaking will reinforce the quality of your writing. It is important that others focus on our message, rather than on the shortcomings in our delivery. Typically, our writing and speaking patterns tend to mirror one another.

Third, be mindful of the words you choose, both in your speech and in your writing. Words mean something, are powerful, and invoke behaviors. Avoid words of battle, such as *battle* itself, or other words that tend to incite and/or excite unnecessarily or unintentionally. Such words are usually inappropriate in and of themselves in such communications. For example, in spite of how competitive our market may be, would we really want to *kill* our competition? These words are incongruent with those of an inspiring, loving, servant leader. If you become really sensitive to not using inappropriate words for the given circumstances, you will instinctively correct yourself prior to uttering them. It will be like describing a spouse as a loving, ruthless, intimate partner. It is difficult to say these words about the same individual, in the same sentence.

As an inspiring, loving, servant leader, using softer words and inflections does not make you a weak person. In actuality, it makes you a stronger person. I am reminded of President Theodore Roosevelt's admonishment, "Speak softly and carry a big stick; you will go far." Even though this maxim has been described as a metaphor for his domestic and foreign policies, I believe it speaks to us as the leaders we desire to be.

After his Presidency, Roosevelt would reflect on these words:

> Persistently the effort has been made to insist that those who advocate keeping our country able to defend its rights are merely adopting 'the policy of the big stick.' In reality, we lay equal emphasis on the fact that *it is necessary to speak softly; in other words, that it is necessary to be respectful toward all people and scrupulously to refrain from wronging them,* while at the same time keeping ourselves in condition to prevent wrong being done to us. (emphasis added)

I became sensitized to the merits of this admonishment at an early age. I remember the incident clearly and it has served as a reminder throughout my life.

I was probably six years old. My mother was a member of The Hillside Extension Club, a group of farm wives who met monthly at one another's homes. During the school year, the children would join their mothers after school at the respective home of the hostess. Not all of the students attended the same school. Alan Pulsky, a bully and a student from another school, would join our little play group of well-behaved and well-intended students. Alan was a couple of years older and delighted in doing whatever he could to infuse unsuspecting fear and panic in the rest of us. He was not a likable kid.

At Christmas time, this women's club would host a family Christmas party at the local community center. The only thing I did not look forward to in attending was the thought of Alan being there.

As an early Christmas present, my aunt from San Diego had mailed a new black pair of engineer boots to me just a couple of days before the big party. I remember being really proud of those boots.

My dad and I were both dressed in our best attire, just waiting for my mom and sister to finish getting ready. In self-admiration of my boots, and as a passing comment, I said, "I can hardly wait for the party. I will be able to kick Alan Pulsky's guts out with my new boots!" It was simply the wrong thing to say, in the wrong place, under the wrong circumstances. All I would remember about the evening were my dad's strong admonishments regarding *such a thing to say* about Alan—and having to stand in the proverbial corner of our little living room for the remaining twenty humiliating minutes, before we left for the party.

These are the reflections I have on those events today. Those were fighting words. Not to plead the fifth, but I do not think I even knew what this expression meant. At the age of six years, I doubt I had a visual of what it would look like to kick someone's guts out. I believe these boots subconsciously provided a false sense of security, power, and protection—and this became my way of expressing it. Why had I not said something more loving and inspirational like, "I wish Alan had a pair of boots like mine"? I must have heard someone else say this, in order to conjure up such a mean-spirited thing to say about another human being, at the age of six—even Alan Pulsky. I never openly blamed him; but to this day, I believe I had probably learned this from Alan.

On a serious note, this is another example of my saying there is always a little good in what appears to be the worst at the time. This memory has been a lifelong reminder that words matter, they have meaning, and words do count.

Lastly, it is also helpful to sense the background, interests, and socio-economic status of the audience and tailor one's delivery accordingly and deliberately. I have never forgotten my rural background, steeped in farming interests. To this day, I am able to adjust my presentation style in such a way as to demonstrate my respect for and understanding of rural, farm life. To borrow an old cliché from the farm, I still know *how to kick "mud" off of my boots.*

Through my entire career, I have worked hard and diligently in focusing on the four recommendations above. Doing so has made me more confident and effective in sharing written and verbal messages with a variety of audiences. I must remain vigilant, however, to avoid the temptation of shortcuts, brevity, and inaccuracies, all resulting in sloppiness and disrespect for others.

6) **We, Us, and Ours versus I, Me, and Mine**

Using *we, us,* and *ours* instead of *I, me,* and *mine* is consistent with promoting an inspiring and loving culture. It also exemplifies the humble nature of genuine servant leadership.

This rule of thumb pertains to both our written and verbal expressions. Choosing inclusive terminology connotes a collective sense of ownership, rather than individual ownership by one individual—the CEO for the sake of discussion. This avoids the impression of one individual taking all of the credit for the actions and accomplishments of a few—or of many. This is another way to emulate the behaviors you expect.

7) **Humbleness, an Ingredient of Servant Leadership**

Always be humble in the presence of others, and they will make you feel valued, *because* you make them feel valued.

Genuine humbleness is an active ingredient and symptom of inspiring, loving, servant leadership.

I liken humbleness in relationships to self-leveling construction materials such as specific caulking and concrete floor leveling products. During the application process, these substances flow into the cracks and crevices, elevating the low places evenly to the height of the highest point. Humbleness has a way of permeating relationships and placing everyone on the same level, at least during the immediate interaction.

Being humble and subscribing to inspiring, loving, servant leadership must not be confused with weakness of character or an inability to make tough decisions. To the contrary, it is a strength of character that seeks fairness, gravitates to doing the right thing, being respectful of others, and yes, making and taking responsibility for tough decisions. It is helpful in developing trustful relationships. Genuine humbleness is not self-serving.

8) Laughter, Good Medicine

Learn to laugh at yourself, reveal yourself to others, and encourage them to laugh with you. Nurture several entertaining self-portrayed examples to share—and that you enjoy sharing.

Laughter, along with the humbleness required to expose oneself, is good medicine that puts your audience (and often the speaker) at ease and allows them to see the human side of you. I have not had any difficulty identifying several such stories about myself, which I call upon frequently. This is one I enjoy sharing about myself:

My college age brother-in-law and his roommates were moving out of their apartment at the end of the school year. They had caused damage to the front door jam and the door itself. Their landlord said he would not charge them for the damages, if they would perform the repairs. My brother-in-law, Rich, asked if I would complete the repairs. I have always considered myself fairly handy, so I said I would repair the damages. We had a plan.

The building had four levels with the front doors facing open balconies. We agreed to meet one afternoon after work to assess the damage and list the needed materials. The next afternoon, after a long day at work for me, I returned to the apartment to complete the repairs. I had packed my tools so I could go directly from work to the apartment. It was a beautiful spring day, which meant I could leave the door open, while completing the repairs.

Eager to get started, I lugged my large toolbox up the stairs to the front door, tapped on the door, and after hearing a faint "come-in," I opened the door and settled-in. I carefully removed my sport coat and tie; and draped them over a near-by sofa; rolled-up my sleeves, and proceeded to empty my toolbox. In doing so, I noticed what appeared to presumably be parents and a son sitting around the television in the far corner of the living room. Having not met Rich's roommates, this did not appear out of the ordinary. I do remember reassuring them the repair would not take very long.

I proceeded to rip into the door jam and door itself. I had removed the trim around the door, along with the locking mechanism. All was proceeding as planned. As I completed these demolition steps, I heard very hearty male laughter coming from the balcony above. This was followed with an urgent admonishment, "Roger, you are in the wrong apartment!"

I remember the proverbial "cold sweat" suddenly running down my chest and the back of my neck and spine. I was quick to tell this patient little group I needed to excuse myself, make some other repairs, and half-heartedly assured them I would be back. I was intrigued to note this door needed the same repairs as that of my brother-in-law.

I quickly replaced the trim around the door and the locking mechanism and exited the premises, with toolbox in one hand and my sport coat and tie in the other—never to return.

This is just one of many personal stories I have collected about myself over the years. I cannot estimate how many times I have told this story in a variety of settings and for different purposes. I hope you enjoyed it as much as I enjoyed sharing it with you. Seldom does a family gathering pass, without Rich initiating a group laughing routine, all in good spirits and welcomed fun.

9) Remember and Visit Often

Everyone has a story. I have intentionally shared much of my own story so you can know and understand me from a total perspective.

Remember where you came from and revisit often. I believe it is always good to revisit one's roots physically, when possible, but I am suggesting something different. It is important for me to not only remember, but to relive the memories of my sheltered formative years and my humble, down-to-earth, well-grounded upbringing.

We are all products of our environments. For me, these revisits remind me to remain humble, to be grateful for those who influenced my early years, to be inspirational and loving to others and to be committed to pay it forward when possible and leave this world just a little better than I found it—both in my personal and professional lives.

10) Never Too Late to Do the Right Thing

I believe it is never too late to *do the right thing*. This applies to a wide variety of circumstances. Perhaps you have needed to reverse a previous decision, as referenced earlier, or maybe, a conversation did not end as you had intended.

Often, these circumstances will call for an apology on your behalf. If you know you have offended someone, particularly in a group setting, apologize and ask for forgiveness immediately. Do not let it leave the room unattended. The offense was made in a pseudo public setting; therefore, the apology should be made in the same setting. Doing so may still require follow-up with the individual in a confidential environment.

This is an important principle for all of us to subscribe to, but it is very important for CEOs and others in leadership roles. If the apology is not made before everyone leaves the room, the hallway conversations after the meeting will be focused not only on what happened, but the individuals will find themselves subconsciously deciding who was right and who was wrong. This is not healthy for an organization committed to building an inspiring, loving culture. If the culture is already tainted, it just contributes to an already unhealthy organization.

Why is this important? For whatever reason, many of us have grown up believing an apology is a sign of weakness. Saying these six words, *"I am sorry, please forgive me,"* is most difficult for some—and very liberating for others. If you've been wrong, simply apologize—and mean it.

Another interesting phenomenon: what is perceived as a sign of weakness by some, will be viewed as a strength in character by many. The news related to the strength of such a plea, will travel quickly throughout the organization. Again, apologizing when you've been wrong is an indication of your humbleness and strength in doing the right thing.

You may be thinking, *"How can I always know if I have offended someone or not?"* The possibility of having offending someone without knowing it is extremely unlikely. If you are perceptive at all, you will know. A pastor of ours once said,

"Even a dog knows when he has done something wrong." How true.

11) People Tell Us Who They Are

I have credited my first wife, Nancy, with several principles of life and living. Here is another: "People tell us who they are without ever muttering a word." She would remind me of this when someone repeatedly disappointed us in demonstrating a breach of confidence, propagating rumors, being untruthful, not taking responsibility for their actions, or not following through on commitments, to name a few. To be on *our* radar, most of the above were already at the level of second-degree infractions.

We believed and agreed everyone deserves at least one sincere opportunity to change. This does beg another question. What is our responsibility to these individuals, with respect to calling them out for these behaviors? In the spirit of demonstrating love for these individuals and building inspirational, loving cultures, I believe we have an obligation to meet with them privately, acknowledge the undesirable behaviors, seek understanding and agreement for improvement, and follow up on a regular basis.

12) Short Distance Between Bedside and Board Room

Jay Upright, PhD, is on my list of mentors. I had just accepted my first CEO position. Before leaving town, Jay invited me to lunch.

After reflecting on our working years together, exchanging updates about our families, reviewing my new job, and sharing other small talk, I said to Jay, "What would be one or two things you would advise me to do, to focus on, in my first CEO position?"

I will always remember his answer, which has served me well all of these years. Jay made very direct eye contact, and said, "Always do what is right for the patient (customer) and you will never make a bad decision, whether in the boardroom or at the patient's bedside." As a non-healthcare example, this could be reworded as "Always do what is right for the customer and you will never make a bad decision, whether in the boardroom or at the customer service desk . . . or on the assembly line."

13) Grandmother's Words of Wisdom

I have already established my love and respect for my paternal grandparents. Now, I will be specific on behalf of my grandmother, Hannah. As a small lad, I remember her spending time with me, just the two of us.

These are a few of the admonishments my grandmother shared with me during our times together:

Always tell the truth. If you tell a lie, you will need to tell twelve other *little white lies* to get out of it. (I have learned you never fully rectify it, regardless of the number.)

Always do your best in everything you do. Any job worth doing is worth doing right.

Always obey your parents. They will always love you, no matter what. They want good things for you. Honor them in return.

Always, if you cannot say something nice about someone, do not say anything at all. All of us have heard a similar version of this admonishment. I admit there were times when I would reflect for long periods of time, without uttering a single word.

Always clean up after yourself. Because I was always trying to make something out of nothing, she would remind me to take good care of my toys, clothes, and the tools I borrowed from our farm workshop.

Always say your prayers and believe in God. She spoke of this often, but her greatest message was found in modeling her faith—the way she lived her life. She was a gentle soul who exhibited a spirit of humility.

Each of you may have similar memories, which have most likely been important to you as guideposts for your lives.

14) Guarded Thoughts and a Predictable Mouth

Carefully guard your thoughts and your mouth will be less likely to assume a direction of its own. As referenced previously, I believe we become what we think about, talk about, dream about, and profess to be important.

I have mentored a young man for several years. Eric is a successful, young executive who excels in most everything he does. He is charismatic, polite, thoughtful, funny, perceptive, presents professionally, and operates at the highest level of integrity. I like and respect Eric a great deal.

We remain in contact, even though he is employed and resides in another major city. It does not happen often during our conversations, but occasionally, when work-life becomes a bit overwhelming for Eric, his extensive vocabulary shrinks to short strings of curse words and other expletives. Even though I do not approve of such language, I am pleased he knows he can go off script with me, as I believe this says something about our relationship.

When this happens, I remind him it is difficult to play by two sets of rules without getting the two accidently crossed-up, which could be embarrassing. In offering this example, I am making three points, (1) if we allow our minds to believe it is okay to use profanity in certain circles and an extensive professional vocabulary in others (work related, for example), then most assuredly, the profanity will slip out when we are least expecting it; (2) a slip in the wrong setting with the wrong audience may be damaging to one's career and/or reputation;

and (3) such language is not characteristic of an inspiring, loving, servant leader.

This is just one example. We could substitute anger outbursts, racial and/or gender slurs, lying, and hundreds of other examples in the above scenario. The risks of a verbal slip can be significant and the outcomes devastating. For the otherwise inspiring individual, it then becomes more difficult to establish an inspirational, loving culture throughout the entire organization.

15) Do Not Worry; Practice Optimism; Be Inspiring

I believe everyone should inspire themselves to be optimistic in all circumstances and eagerly model optimism to others. Others will become inspired by how you react in all circumstances, good or bad. They will take strength from you and your example. Reflecting on the Pebble Theory, we may never know to what extent our example penetrates the lives of others.

Optimism, in my opinion, is a learned behavior. The choice is ours, we can either see the glass as half-full or half-empty. I choose to see it as half-full. For me, optimism is rooted more deeply and emanates from my personal philosophy to not worry. When we worry, I believe we are telling God we are not confident He will take care of (or is capable of taking care of) our circumstances.

In Philippians 4: 6–7 (NIV), we are told, "Do not be anxious about anything, but in everything, by prayer and petition, with thanksgiving, present your requests to God. And the peace of God, which transcends all understanding, will guard your hearts and your minds in Christ Jesus." Please hear me clearly in saying, "It is not easy for me to not worry, I often need to guard my every thought." It is one thing to *profess* and yet another to *practice*.

We cannot be Pollyanna about this either, and just say, *"Everything will be fine; God will take care of this for me,"* without any effort on our part. God equips us with good minds and bodies and an ability to explore, to reason, and to make choices, all for the purpose of making the right and most appropriate decisions affecting ourselves and others. I recommend always being optimistic but truthful, even though the truth may be difficult to deliver.

Another interesting property of optimism is that it *rules in* rather than *rules out*. When making personal or group decisions, an optimistic approach, coupled with an optimistic atmosphere, will provide license to consider a wide-range of possibilities and options from which to choose.

Creating such an optimistic atmosphere and facilitating open, optimistic discussions is the leader's responsibility. The leader sets the tone and expectations, and the group is responsible to follow suit. From this process, the leader and the group will be satisfied the final decision is the best one, given the circumstances at the time.

I contend there is power in not worrying, practicing optimism, and being inspiring and loving to others. Interestingly, these are humble behaviors that produce powerful outcomes.

16) Emulate Behaviors You Expect

Inspire others to emulate the positive behaviors you expect in yourself. I am reminded of the old adage, *A picture is worth a thousand words.* Another also comes to mind, *Practice what you preach.* If we want to be inspiring and loving to others, our actions must be inspirational to others—and we must speak inspirationally; in doing so, we reinforce our actions with our words and our words with our actions.

One of the worst things we can do is to profess one thing and practice the opposite. Inspiration is only effective when it is built on solid beliefs. We must first believe it is important in our minds, hearts, and souls—and then it will become second nature. We become what we think about, talk about, dream about, and profess to be important. Credibility is an invaluable attribute to be coveted.

We want our words and actions to provide license for those of others. One of the most gratifying things for me as a CEO is to witness and hear board members, members of the leadership team, the management staff, and staff repeat to others (within and outside of the organization) what I had said and done; utilizing the same verbiage, phrases, examples, stories, and inflections I have shared in establishing and promoting a culture characterized with inspirational, loving, servant leadership. I also enjoy witnessing the pride they demonstrate on behalf of one another and the organization.

17) Play Your Best On and Off the Field

Inspire yourself to always play your best on and off the field. I am focusing significant time on the field—on the organizations we represent. Of equal importance, is how we play off the field—how do we present at home as a spouse, a parent, or other family member? Are we inspiring and loving to our families? What are we like as members of our community service organization? How do we behave at the athletic club, both as we win and as we lose? How do others see us in our places of worship? How do we behave when we are out on the town, with or without family? Perhaps the best litmus test is this: What do others see when we are at athletic events and our team is losing?

Inspire yourself to be the same inspirational, loving person off the field as you profess to be on the field at work. Operate with one set of rules and a single playbook, maintain the same personal expectations, and produce consistent results that bring honor to those around you, to yourself, and to the entire organization that depends on your leadership. Everyone deserves your best.

As a general guideline, aside from legal human resource requirements, do not employ expectations at work you would not consider doing at home.

I enjoy hearing commendable tributes about individuals, while they are still alive. When Eli Manning retired in January, 2020, the headline in our local newspaper read, "Giants' Manning Retires After 16 Seasons." John Mara, the Giants' president and chief executive officer, shared this quote, "For 16 seasons, Eli Manning defined what it is to be a New York Giant *on and off the field* . . .. He represented our franchise as a *consummate professional with dignity and accountability.*" *(emphasis added)*

18) Good in What Appears to Be the Worst

Inspire yourself to believe there is always a little good in what appears to be the worst at the time. I contend this is true in most, if not all circumstances. Though sometimes, we really need to look hard to identify the *little good.*

This is consistent with the discussion regarding *optimism* above. I also find this admonishment helpful as a reminder to be thankful for our many blessings, whether large or small.

Most of us have times when it feels like the world is caving in on us and the burden is too great to carry. Such circumstances may be confined to work, home, or just plain living. Whenever I find myself slipping into my little pity party, I complete an exercise that moves my needle back into the normal range. Either in writing or mentally in my head, I deliberately prepare and review the list of items I am thankful for and blessed to have. I have never counted all of the items, but by the time I reach twenty or twenty-five, I am feeling much better. I believe this is one way God reminds me how much He loves and cares for me.

19) Knack-Knack; What's There

Be inspired to develop *knacks* for certain methods in thinking, planning processes, completing specific tasks, and being intuitive about specific situations, circumstances, and timing. I've found this section to be one of the hardest to prepare, describe, and discuss. I am reminded of the proverbial rose, as it is difficult to describe, but I definitely recognize when I see it. How many times, when describing another person, have you heard someone say, "They just have a knack for doing such and such." The dictionary tells us *knack* is "an acquired or natural skill at performing a task, a tendency to do something."

I believe *knacks* can be God-given skills and talents; however, I also believe these tendencies can become learned behaviors. If developed and employed effectively, *knacks* can be very powerful. Honing these knacks will make you more affective and effective:

a) Develop a knack for putting people at ease.

In previous sections, I have discussed employing humor about yourself, demonstrating good listening skills, calling people by their first names, focusing genuine interest in someone and their families; learning something specific about individuals and remembering it, and coming alongside of someone doing their job.

I add the following:

1) Always wear a smile—unless circumstances at the time make it inappropriate to do so. This also applies to good telephone etiquette, as perceptive people can hear a smile.

2) When speaking with another individual or a small group, always strive to make as much direct eye contact as possible. Our eyes are the glass doors to our souls.

3) Always strive to be the first to smile, acknowledge, and greet, as you approach one another. Even if you are speaking with someone else in the hallway, it is generally

appropriate to do so, as the other person passes by. As you become proficient at doing this, you will be able to honor both individuals, without either feeling they have been overlooked through distraction.

4) If you do need to interrupt a conversation with someone, remember the last thing that was being said when interrupted, so you can honor the individual by picking-right-up where you left off, without having to ask them, "Where were we?"

b) Develop a knack for good timing and reading others.

The overall goal here is to say, do, or present something at the very best time, in order to maximize opportunities for effectiveness and success. This is important, as you may only have one opportunity to get it right.

One of the challenges in developing this knack is knowing when it is or is not a good time. Since we are usually dependent on people in order to maximize these so-called opportunities, we need to predict, or sense, when it is the best time for these individuals. Doing so is also an opportunity to demonstrate respect and honor for others.

I consistently employ a couple of helpful hints that have served me well over the years. First, if possible, I always prefer (and suggest) meeting with individuals face-to-face, as this non-verbal language provides me with another dimension. In this age of global markets, social media, long-distance relationships, and mobile span-of-influence, this is not always feasible or possible. Video conferencing and the telephone become the next best options.

Second, if I am calling someone on the telephone, I will begin by greeting them by name and identifying myself. Usually, by this time, I already have a hint whether or not this will be a good time.

This is key, I always ask if they have a few minutes to visit or if I am calling at a bad time. Their response will determine my next steps. If they indicate it is fine, I will promise to be respectful of their time, initiate a bit of small talk, and get to the point of my call. If there is any hesitation or they appear to be hurried, I will ask when I may be able to call them back. Unless life or limb are threatened, I have found it best to postpone.

It is disappointing to me that a small percentage of my callers provide this gesture to me. I find it annoying when callers lunge into the conversation abruptly and continue non-stop. I become more focused on my annoyance with their lack of consideration than I am on the intended purpose of their call. It is their missed opportunity to demonstrate respect for another individual and their time.

c) **Develop a knack for identifying priorities and having a plan.**

It has been said, *Life is a matter of priorities.* There is truth in this adage, as we are constantly determining priorities, both consciously with deliberation—and subconsciously, without much thought. This is important because how we process priorities determines the decisions we make, and the decisions we make affect others.

With significant decisions, I advocate for seeking counsel before making the final decision—if time permits. Since priorities and decisions go hand in hand, you will be called upon to mentor and maneuver others in establishing subsequent priorities for implementation, personally or professionally. This is why this inherent skill and ability will be critical to you, to others, and to the organization or your family.

Linked to this inherent ability to identify priorities, is my recommendation to always have at least one contingency plan. Depending on the nature of the plan, you will need to decide the level of involvement with others, the formality of the processes, the extent of the "need to know," and the public versus private knowledge.

As the CEO, regardless of the above considerations, I have made it a practice to have at least one contingency plan in mind, based on the *What-Ifs*. Doing so, has allowed me to continue challenging the original plan and to react spontaneously with necessary adjustments. I have taken pride in assuring myself that *"I always have a plan."*

d) Develop a knack for paying attention to your instincts.

Some might describe this as a *hunch*, which is defined as "a feeling or guess based on intuition rather than known facts." *Intuition* is defined as "a thing that one knows or considers likely from instinctive feeling rather than conscious reasoning." One such expression, we often hear is, *"I do not know why, but I just had a feeling about . . .."*

I have worked with many physicians during my career who represented a wide variety of medical disciplines. I do not remember the topic during a hallway conversation with one of our more colorful cardiologists, but I do remember how he affirmed his position on the particular matter.

As he held his left hand out, palm-up, fingers widely-spread, he repeatedly jabbed his open palm with his right index finger, looked directly into my eyes, and emphatically said, "When you have something that looks like a dead fish and smells like a dead fish, it is probably a dead fish." I generally pride myself in having one of the last words in any conversation, but his analogy had totally disarmed me, as he had made his point. This was his way of convincing me that he had a very strong *hunch* about something being true.

I had the privilege of working with this capable physician for several more years. In addition to being known as a cutting-edge cardiologist, he had a characteristic grin and twinkle in his eye. During subsequent group meetings, we would occasionally share a light moment when he would capture my

attention, point to his open palm, and display that characteristic grin and twinkle in his eyes. Point well-taken.

20) Be a Risk-Taker

Inspire yourself to be a risk-taker—*with calculation.* If you
do not train yourself to this mindset, you will find yourself
moving too deliberately and slowly; thus, missing many opportunities on behalf of the organization you were hired to
inspire. Advocation for always having an original plan, and
one or more contingency plans, is also applicable.

The key phrase is *with calculation.* One of my mentors,
Mr. Dale Johnson, would remind us to *go slowly,* so we *could go
fast.* I believe this is what he was describing at the time. He was
reminding us to be inclusive of others, deliberate in planning,
to minimize the risk, and respond to the market quickly with
confidence and fortitude.

Dale was an inspiring, loving, servant leader who impacted the lives of many through his humble, compassionate approach to those he worked with, on behalf of the organization
he was called to serve.

21) Business of Building Collaborative Relationships

Most of us, when asked what type of business we are in,
respond with a one- to two-word response, such as banking,
real estate, farming, or sales.

When asked, I would respond with *healthcare;* however, I
would follow up by saying, "Our basic underlying business is
one of building collaborative relationships. It is one thing for
two or more parties to agree to be cooperative, but it is quite
another to agree to co-labor, to lock arms for a common cause
or purpose. Good things fall out of good relationships."

I utilized this response and explanation many times during
my career when referring to patients, families, employees,
vendors, professionally-related organizations, and community

organizations. This is a good approach to use in *establishing* a level playing field between and amongst parties. It also establishes a prior commitment to agreed-upon mutual behaviors, going forward. Stephen R. Covey reminds us "Relationships move at the speed of trust." Trust is a key component of any relationship, personal or professional.

I was blessed to be the CEO ultimately responsible for the construction of a new hospital and a major associated renovation project several years ago. This is an experience every healthcare CEO should have at least one time during their professional career.

Referring to this simply as *construction* is a gross understatement as the entire project required conceptual plans, feasibility studies, community information meetings, necessary local and state approvals, financing, architectural drawings, interior designs, furbishing plans, a ground-breaking ceremony, actual *construction*, punch lists, a dedication/open house ceremony, and occupancy of the new/renovated structures.

At the beginning of the entire process, I met face-to-face with the General Contractor's Project Director and shared my philosophy of the hospital being in the basic business of *building collaborative relationships* at all levels. He was quick to agree, and together, on behalf of both of our organizations, we forged this understanding as our performance pledge to one another. We would function as one large team with a common interest—to build a new hospital and renovate portions of the old.

As a next step, the Project Director and I co-facilitated a meeting comprised of representatives of the hospital and the general contractor's team. During this meeting, we discussed and modeled our mutually-agreed unity from the onset. In doing so, we outlined our commitments to and our expectations of one another.

This became the Project Team and every individual team member agreed we would function as one large team, and not two or more separate teams, going forward. As additional agencies and sub-contractors became engaged in the various construction segments, the Project Team would meet with these groups and emphasize that they too, were now joining this one large team. Additionally, we would jointly emphasize the expected behaviors of all team members and our process-es for making decisions. We would then provide some light moments by referring to their *required initiation ceremonies,* which reinforced camaraderie amongst the team members.

I share this story for a specific purpose. The entire process, from concept development through occupancy, spanned two and a half years, plus another two years through the warranty period and beyond. This was a $30 million project, which was completed on time and under budget. The result was a beauti-ful new facility with complementary renovated spaces, which the community is extremely proud of to this day.

Mutually, we agreed to a number of change orders as a Project Team. The team had several serious discussions, but we settled every issue by consensus. Never once, was there any threat of litigation or need for third-party mediation. Having such an experience in this highly competitive, often cut-throat, litigious work environment is almost an anomaly. I credit such outcomes to the commitment we made to one another early on that our basic business underlying the construction of a new hospital was to build a highly collaborative relationship and function as one large team—not two or more.

The general contractor provided a two-year warranty period, effective upon completion of the final punch list and occupancy of the building. To the credit of the general con-tractor, they were still completing incidental repairs for an-other two years following expiration of the original warranty. This serves as a testimony to our relationship. To this day, the construction company knows they may provide my name as a reference to prospective customers and that I will provide an excellent reference, with emphasis on how we managed our project as one large team—and not two.

I encourage the adoption of this basic philosophy for everyone on my intended audience list. This is a valuable approach in establishing and nurturing all relationships.

Once you subscribe to this as a philosophy, it is important to speak of this commitment often, as it will become embedded in the minds of staff members, other individuals, and staff of outside organizations. It will become an expectation to live by. We must first believe in the philosophy and be willing to be held accountable to a higher standard, or it will be not be effective, personally or organizationally.

22) Bull versus Bear

I encourage each of you to be inspired to *pull others up* rather *than claw them down*. To illustrate this point, I have borrowed the bull and bear symbols embedded in stock market jargon. The term *bull* or *bullish* comes from the bull, who strikes upwards with its horns, thus pushing prices (people in this illustration) higher. The term *bear* or *bearish* comes from the bear, who strikes downward with its paws, thus pushing prices (people in this illustration) down.

Let us recall several principles:

First, God has created each of us with unique skills, talents, and interests.

Second, God also has a special plan for each of our lives. He has created and set us apart for specific purposes, heavenly-assigned duties, and responsibilities.

Third, as CEOs and others in servant leadership roles, it is our job to identify and uncover these talents and skills, and to enhance, encourage, and support as necessary; thus, inspiring these individuals to engage in meaningful measures with others, on behalf of the organizations we serve—and their families. When this happens, it is a wonderful thing to witness.

Putting these three principals into practice should be accomplished in a loving manner. It *may* mean supporting a process and plan different from your own. It *will likely mean* accepting ultimate accountability for outcomes, without taking any of the credit for the accomplishment. It *will mean* pushing others up, rather than clawing them down.

I refer to the process or committing to these principals as *the more inspiring and loving we are to others, the more inspired and loving we become.* Some of you will recognize this as a play on the old cliché, "The more power you give away, the more powerful you become." Referencing this cliché does not mean I subscribe to its usage, as I do not.

For me, power and inspiration are like oil and water, they do not mix well, and they certainly are not the same. I prefer to replace *power* with *inspiration* and *powerful* with *inspired*, to read "The more *inspiration* you give away, the more *inspired* you become." Abraham Lincoln expressed it this way, "When I do good, I feel good, and when I do bad, I feel bad, and that's my religion."

23) Do Not Tolerate Incompetence; Replace It

From this sub-title, you may presume I am recommending termination of incompetent employees. Even though this may be in the future of some, this is not the primary premise of this section.

To the contrary, termination should not be considered unless we have exhausted all reasonable options within defined timelines—or the individual has done something so egregious we have no choice but to terminate. I recommend we replace incompetency with competency—in a loving, inspirational manner. Do not tolerate incompetency, replace it, and build on it.

Prior to receiving her MBA degree and becoming an executive with a major midwestern insurance company, Mary Lou, the second love of my life, was a practicing dental hygienist; taught at the school of dentistry; was a part-time instructor at a local university; and had served as a Central Region Dental Hygiene Examiner for a number of years.

Mary Lou tells of the afternoon she was lamenting her disappointment in one of her students for repeated ineptness, with Dr. Ahrens, Mary Lou's mentor. Having listened patiently while Mary Lou expressed her frustration, Dr. Ahrens paused and said, "Mary Lou, do you know what your problem is?" In response, Mary Lou said, "No, but I believe I am about ready to find out." Dr. Ahrens smiled and said, "Your problem, Mary Lou, is you do not tolerate incompetency." She likes to tell this story; not only to make a point, but to honor Dr. Ahrens, who she respected a great deal.

I encourage all CEOs, and others in leadership positions, to be inspired and committed to *raising the competency bar* within the organization. Each of you will find yourself in one of two positions. Either you have been with the organization for a significant period of time or you are new to the organization. In either position, this is one of the best investments you can make on behalf of the organization. Remember, it starts with you. Perhaps, you have made this commitment to yourself and others already.

There are two opportunities to enhance the overall competency of staff within an organization. One is to individually and collectively *push up* the current staff and the other is to hire well for *all* new and replacement positions. These two approaches can and should be orchestrated in tandem.

I cannot overemphasize the importance of hiring well, which is commonly referenced but not always practiced effectively.

This segment will focus on the first of these two opportunities—raising the bar of the current staff, individually and collectively. Your job is to first, inspire yourself and then, inspire all others within the organization with (1) a desire to be better, (2) the gratification of being better, and (3) the commitment to become better and better and better, without limits. Remember, Joe Tye tells us, "When a movement reaches the 30 percent tipping point, we could not reverse the forward progress if we tried to do so."

Following are several principles for your review and consideration. If you are to be genuine in your beliefs with others, deliberate as a servant leader, and successful in promoting an inspirational culture, these are must-haves and must-dos:

1) If you are new to the organization, develop an initial, informal assessment of how the organization has been operating—what is the culture like now and why? One approach is to meet individually with a variety of individuals representing a wide spectrum of positions throughout the organization. As a perceptive individual, you will be able to determine this within a short time. From this assessment, commit to building an inspirational, loving culture.

2) Believe with conviction, that we (as individuals and organizations) become what we think about, talk about, dream about, and profess to be important.

3) Make a practice of providing the benefit of doubt whenever you can.

4) Remember, *everyone* has a story.

5) Everyone deserves at least one sincere opportunity (and maybe more) to change.

6) Believe every position, and every person in these positions, is important; therefore, inspire and love these individuals in equal measure.

7) Be in the business of *growing people* and the organization will follow suit.

8) Build confidence in the organization. Help everyone in the organization come to believe in themselves, in one another, and in the organization.

9) We do not always know what staff are dealing with in their personal lives. Even though it may not be any of our business, we should still care, be cognizant, and make accommodations, if possible. Why? Because each member of the organization is a creature of God—and personal life affects work life and vice versa. We employ total individuals, not just the work-related portions of their lives.

10) Emulate the behaviors you expect—today, if this is your first day with the organization; or today, if this is the day you've committed to becoming more inspirational and loving in your current position. We all have *first* days.

11) Understand and believe that inspiring, loving, servant leadership is not to be confused with being weak. To the contrary, it is synonymous with being strong. You will still be called upon to make tough decisions, but you will feel more objective and confident as an inspired, loving, servant leader.

12) Believe and remember that *inspiration* (love-based) gathers and *motivation* (fear-based) scatters.

The primary focus so far has been on doing everything possible to move the incompetent to competent, either in their current position or another position for which they are better suited. There are nevertheless times when, in spite of our best efforts, there will be times when we will not be successful with either of these two efforts.

If the person is to be transferred to another position, it must be because they have successfully competed for the new position through normal application channels, and they have not been transferred without discretion. We must refrain from taking what *appears to be* the path of least resistance, or simply transferring the problems along with the individual to another area. I contend this is not only unfair to the receiving department, it is not fair to the individual either. It is also unfair to the organization leadership serves, which has failed to recover the significant investment that it has made in the employee.

Previously, I've made the case for replacing incompetency with competency. When all efforts have failed, we will need to move the incompetent individual out of the organization. Before this occurs, as inspiring, loving, servant leaders, we must be satisfied we have exhausted all reasonable attempts to preserve the human being and the human *spirit*. I refer to this state of mind as having your *banner* of justice strapped on with complete confidence you are doing the right thing for all parties—the organization, the department, and yes, the employee.

Some things are worth *struggling* over and through, to reach the decision that is best for everyone involved. Share this sentiment with your leadership team and have them know it is okay to *struggle* with certain decisions, in our attempts to be as compassionate as possible—as individuals and organizations. This needs to be elevated to a posture of strength and not perceived weakness. After all, we are striving to be inspiring, *loving,* servant leaders.

There is a tipping point when it becomes more unfair to the employee to tolerate incompetent behaviors in a miserable environment, than it is to move them out of the organization. Be assured, as hard as it may be, inspiring, loving, servant leaders can manage these circumstances to the extent that even the potentially-aggrieved employee recognizes the merits of the decision. This is *management by the heart at its best.*

On a positive note, vividly imagine the fun in leading an organization comprised of individuals whose opinions are sought and respected, who know their work is important, who feel valued, believe they are properly armed to do their jobs, know you believe in them, and enjoy dreaming and thriving in an inspirational, loving culture. Then, imagine the fun each employee will be capable of experiencing in this inspirational, loving culture—and the legacy you will have left for staff, their families, and the organization.

This quote by John Quincy Adams reinforces this discussion well: "If your actions inspire others to dream more, learn more, do more and become more, you are a leader."

24) Praise Publicly and Criticize Privately

As an inspiring, loving, servant leader, you will seek opportunities to praise individual and group accomplishments frequently; however, you will despise the need to criticize others—ever. If, and when, criticism is required, it is also our responsibility to deliver the message in the most effective manner. I do not know what the scientific proportion should be in a highly inspirational culture; nor do I know, what is an acceptable proportion. As the CEO, or anyone in a leadership role, you are responsible for addressing both in a timely fashion.

I do know the operational ratio should be something like a 100:1 ratio—100 praises for every one criticism, rather than 1:1. I have tracked various data points during my career, but I have never found it necessary to track praises and criticisms, nor should you. You will just know.

I am amused when I hear someone speak of the need to provide *constructive* criticism. Perhaps, referring to it as *destructive* criticism; or at best, *renovative* criticism would be more appropriate. Even if delivered by the most eloquent and diplomatic of individuals, any type of criticism is received as criticism. We must remember to not break the spirit of another individual.

The primary thrust of this segment is to emphasize the importance of praising in public settings (with others present) and criticizing in private settings (with no others present). The purpose in both settings is to honor the dignity of another human being.

There will be times, in a meeting for example, when one or more individuals will say or do something you believe requires a response that could appear critical in nature. You will need to provide some response. What do you do and say? Everyone else, as bystanders, will be watching to see how you will handle the situation. You will need to decide spontaneously.

Given the multitude of topics and circumstances, it is impossible to describe one response that will fit all situations. If it does not feel right to discuss it within the group at the time, one can always suggest the issue be addressed outside of the group setting. As the leader, not responding or responding inappropriately would be a lost opportunity; and responding appropriately, will be an opportunity seized. How you handle any given situation should be a teaching moment for everyone present, regardless of their positions on the issue.

25) No Intimidation Without Permission

Regarding potentially disruptive comments during meetings, it is appropriate to share another personal insight. All of us, especially leaders, should be equipped and prepared to respond to such comments in an inspiring, loving manner—all in such a manner as to produce teaching moments for the testifiers and the witnesses alike.

I am reminded of a comment Mr. Ron Wachter, one of my mentors, shared from time to time. He would say, "No one can intimidate you unless you allow them to do so." He was advocating for skillful disarmament; rather than an exchange of fire in responding to potentially caustic comments.

26) Commit to Nothing Illegal, Unethical, or Immoral

Everyone has assertions they believe in, adopt as their own, and utilize as guideposts in daily living—hopefully, these are consistently utilized in both their personal and professional lives. Inspiring, loving, servant leaders have one playbook for both.

I've shared several of these *Rogerisms* throughout the book. This is one I have adhered to for most of my life and one which has served me well along with organizations I have served: *Commit publicly to never doing anything illegal, unethical, or immoral*—as an individual and an organization. This is especially important for the CEO, other leaders, and aspiring leaders.

The most important thing is that you personally believe this, commit to living your life around this belief, and model the associated behaviors consistently. It is also important to share this commitment publicly. In doing so, you are inviting others to hold you to this high standard. Commitment to these principles will produce a high degree of personal credibility and trust.

This will become a standard for the organization you are responsible for and/or represent. You will know you have penetrated the culture of the organization when you hear others repeating this as though they are claiming it for themselves and the organization.

We have already discussed a first cousin to the above: *It is never too late to do the right thing.* You will find a great deal of purpose, commitment, credibility, and strength through public commitment and effective modeling of these two assertions—separately and together.

27) Recognize Mentors While They Are Living

All of us have individuals who have been influential and instrumental in our lives. Many of these individuals are considered personal and professional mentors. I, like each of you, have a list of these individuals. Throughout this manuscript, I refer to several of these individuals, who are on my list of mentors.

For three reasons I recommend we recognize and acknowledge these individuals, while they are still living:

First, it is a loving, respectful, gesture to honor individuals who have positively impacted our lives significantly.

Second, it serves as a humbling reminder that my accomplishments are not entirely mine alone, as God has placed many individuals in my life who have significantly impacted who I am, where I have been, and where I anticipate going.

Third, it serves as a reminder of how important it is that our names are listed as mentors on the lists of others who follow us in this journey we call *life* and *living*. What is more important and lasting than having made a positive effect on someone else's life? What an important investment this is—investing our time and talents in others. It is a good time to reference the *Pebble Theory*.

Previously, I introduced you to Mr. Norval (Mac) McCaslin, my high school vocational agriculture instructor, Future Farmers of America (FFA) Advisor, and one of my favorite teachers. He is also on my list of mentors. There will be some overlap between these references to Mr. McCaslin, but I have two distinct purposes for sharing the separate accounts.

Mr. McCaslin was instrumental in steering my decision to go on to college. Nancy and I chose Mr. McCaslin and his wife, Barb, to be the host and hostess at our wedding. As I look back on our days together, I remain fond of him and appreciative of the personal interest he invested in me.

Following high school graduation, through my college years, and early into my career, I had visited with Mr. McCaslin from time to time. On each of these occasions, I recall telling him how much I appreciated everything he had done for me.

Life happens, and over a period of several years, we had both moved geographically. After I had graduated from high school, the McCaslins moved from my home community in pursuit of first, Mr. McCaslin's doctorate degree and then, a faculty appointment at a major midwestern university, where they remained for the rest of his career. As we moved farther apart geographically, we also visited less frequently.

I regretted not making more of an effort to remain in contact with Mr. McCaslin (Mac). (Even in my adult years, following graduation, I still found it uncomfortable to refer to him as Mac when I was visiting with him personally.)

More years passed—it had been several years since we had spoken. I found myself thinking of Mac and recalling favorite memories. This occurred at various times over a period of approximately three weeks. I would remind myself I needed to call Mac, update him on my career and family, and learn more about his family; and most importantly, tell him one more time how much I respected him and how grateful I remained for everything he had done for me during those early years.

Finally, one evening before it became too late to call, I telephoned Mac to visit with him. The telephone rang several times before being answered by his wife, Barb. I identified myself, and, of course, Barb was so gracious in acknowledging and remembering me. After some small talk, I asked if I could visit with Mac.

There was this long pause in her response; during which, I found myself preparing for what I was about to hear. Her voice trembled a bit, as she proceeded to tell me Mac had died two weeks earlier. After extending our condolences, I shared my primary purpose for my call. She was most grateful to be reminded of my appreciation and respect for Mac (Mr. McCaslin).

I was immediately overcome with guilt and regret—and asking myself, *"Why had I not called when I was first prompted in thought for him and his family?"* At that moment, I vowed to remind my mentors from time to time how much I have appreciated them as individuals and mentors and for the differences they have made in my life. I do not want to miss another opportunity to tell them personally, before it is too late.

Coupled with this is another commitment I have made to myself: If I find myself being prompted in thought about someone, I will attempt to contact them as soon as possible. Sometimes we do not know what people are dealing with personally. There have been times in my life when a telephone call or personal note has arrived at the perfect time. No doubt this has happened to each of you, as well.

In reviewing N.L. "Mac" McCaslin's obituary a few days later, there, amidst the long list of employment appointments, professional organizations, academic achievements, and various honors, I was struck with this one sentence, "Mac's passion was teaching and mentoring graduate students." I can only trust, unlike me, many of these individuals honored Mac one more time before he died with a telephone call, a note, or a personal visit expressing their respect and appreciation for the differences he had no doubt made in their lives.

28) Wear a Smile Unless It Doesn't Complement the Setting

Our non-verbal communication often speaks as loudly, if not more loudly, than our verbal communication. In order to soften our demeanor, I suggest we maintain a smile and direct eye contact as much as possible—providing it is not inconsistent with the existing environment. For example, wearing a big, mouth-widening smile may not be appropriate during a funeral service.

A smile exudes a sense of calmness, confidence, and compassion—the three Cs. I also contend it affects the tone of our voice; thus, prompting the suggestion one should smile when answering and visiting on the telephone. We tend to sound more pleasant and accommodating when we smile and couple it with direct eye contact.

I am reminded of two adages: First, *Our eyes are windows to the soul,* credited to Shakespeare; the second, *Words tell and emotions sell.* The inspiring, loving, servant leader recognizes the power of words and emotion and will project both with a sense of sincerity, genuine interest, appropriateness for the moment, and a caring and accommodating attitude. I am thankful God set us apart with the gifts of memory and emotion.

As a child growing up on the farm, I remember there were times I would be called upon by my parents to apologize to my younger brother and/or sisters for some innocent shortcoming.

I would extend my heartfelt apology and my parents would say something to the effect of, "You didn't sound like you meant it," or "That didn't sound like a sincere apology," or "Say it like you mean it." Most likely, I had said it with a smile on my face. This was a situation where my words didn't tell *and* my emotions didn't sell.

STOKING THE FIRE WITH WOOD

Before venturing into the next chapter, "Fanning The Flame—Inspire Others," I will share several experiences I had early in my career, which have impacted my convictions through the years:

1) General Eisenhower's Take On Leadership
During the summer between my junior and senior years in high school, I attended a leadership camp sponsored by the Future Farmers of America (FFA). Since I had been an officer within the organization and had recently been elected president for my senior year, I was expected to attend this conference. As I look back on this experience, I identify it as my first exposure to thinking about *leadership* through an organized approach. I do not remember many of the finer details of the conference, but I will always remember General Eisenhower's definition of leadership, "Leadership is the art of getting someone else to do something you want done because he wants to do it." I find it interesting that General Eisenhower said "leadership is the *art* of . . ." Webster's definition of *art* in this usage, is "skill acquired by experience, study, or observation." I am confident General Eisenhower mastered each of these three areas, all of which

made him a renowned General and subsequently, the Commander and Chief, and our thirty-fourth president of the United States.

I have shared this many times since those early days. I believe the present-day editorial update should be, "*Inspirational, loving, servant* leadership is the art of inspiring someone else to do something you want done because he/she *is inspired* to do it.*"* I am taking the liberty, on behalf of General/President Eisenhower, to submit that I believe Mr. Eisenhower would not only approve, but endorse these small, but significant present-day enhancements.

2) The Three TLC Choices

We all have *three choices* when we find ourselves in an unsettling culture, environment, or relationship. For our purposes, this discussion will center on work environments or organizational cultures. Generally speaking, much of what I propose could also be aimed at unhealthy relationships in our personal lives. I refer to these three options as the *TLC Choices.* The traditional meaning of *TLC* "Tender Loving Care" for ourselves is applicable here, as unhealthy work environments can be menacing to our mental and physical health. Sadly, since many of us spend more time at work than we do with our own family members, we should feel obligated to exercise our choices, rather than mortgage our health for uninspiring work environments.

If we are in an uninspiring work environment, we can choose to <u>T</u>olerate (stuff it *down*) the situation, <u>L</u>eave (exit *out* of) the organization, or <u>C</u>hange (manage *up*) the environment, or culture, of the organization. Your first reaction may be *"easier said than done"* with each of these choices. There may be challenging circumstances, which will make any or all of these difficult to accomplish.

I was halfway through my third semester in college when I came to the realization that I needed to find another job besides the busboy job I had at the fraternity. My funds from the liquidation of my high school farming interests were evaporating. Being the oldest of four children, I was on my own from this point forward. To my dad's credit, he had helped me accumulate livestock and farming assets, which when sold, financed my first full year and half of my third semester. Through a friend who knew a friend, I was introduced to a job at Bryan Memorial Hospital as a respiratory therapist. I have often mused when I graduated from high school, when people would ask me what I wanted to be, to do with my life, my pat answer became: "I do not know what I will end up doing; however, I know there are two things I will never do: one is being a mortician and the other is anything related to hospitals." Lesson learned: never say never, as this would mark the beginning of my over-fifty-year career in healthcare.

The individual who hired me apologetically said he could only offer me the job at $1.50 per hour. Little did he know how pleased I was with this wage, as I had been hauling hay bales and scooping corn to the shellers all summer in high-humidity temperatures for $1.25 per hour. He also told me he preferred hiring college students, and when the patient care for the shift was completed, we could study. It did not take long for me to conclude the director's casual approach was being misinterpreted by several of the staff. Therapy was being cut short, therapist–patient interactions were not always patient-centered, patient documentation was inconsistent and lacking, charges were not captured accurately, equipment was not being adequately cleaned, patient teaching was insufficient, supplies were out of stock, and more. College studies, however, appeared to be flourishing.

I appreciated this job for a variety of reasons. I felt fortunate to have a job with flexible hours in a clean, environmentally-controlled setting. I was learning a great deal about medicine, patient care, and enjoyed working with the staff. But one looming problem was the confliction I was beginning to feel. Our primary purpose as a department was to address and treat the needs of the patients. This was not happening consistently, due to self-interests and lack of an inspiring, loving, department culture. Overall performance was maintenance at best without a collective desire to be better, to become better and better. Feeling inadequate, deceitful, and unworthy by association was troubling to me. In reflection, I would now describe my diagnosis as a lack of an inspiring, loving, servant leader environment or culture.

In retrospect, I had three TLC choices at the time: I could *tolerate* the situation, *leave* the organization, or attempt to *change* the culture. I was already conflicted, so tolerating current conditions was not appealing. I did not want to leave the organization as I absolutely needed the job. Tuition had to be paid, along with board and room and necessary miscellaneous expenses. Given my need for a paying job, this simply was not an option. I was nineteen years old and had been with the organization for six months when I chose the last option, to change the culture.

I decided to prepare a written proposal, which I presented to the director of the respiratory therapy department. These are the things I remember about the proposal. I identified these sections in the proposal: "Introduction/Purpose Statement," "List of Current Issues/Deficiencies," "Proposal," "Conditions of Support," and "Summary." I contacted the director to schedule a private meeting with him, making sure I would have an adequate amount of his time.

With minor changes, depending on the topic, I have generally followed a similar outline throughout the years. I make a point of scheduling private meetings, ensuring an adequate amount of time for presentation and discussion. Though some of the finer details have escaped, I will always remember the conditions I outlined in the proposal section, as follows:

1) I asked to assume responsibility for full supervision of the department;
2) I asked for the director's unconditional support of my supervision;
3) I asked for a trial period of six months;
4) I said I did not want an official title, initially;
5) I said I did not want a pay adjustment, initially;
6) I did ask permission to have a varied and flexible schedule, which would allow me to be present throughout the

twenty-four hours, seven days per week on an unannounced, come and go basis; and

7) Given the above, if he (the director) liked what he saw at the end of the six-month period, he would formalize the position, create a corresponding job title, and implement an appropriate pay adjustment, aligning with the responsibilities of the position.

Another thing I learned from this experience, is to *always* make it as easy as possible for the other party to say yes. The director agreed to everything I had proposed and requested. The rest is history. At the end of the six-month period, he kept his word and honored our agreement by formalizing the position, assigning a job title reflective of my supervisory responsibilities, and established a fair rate of pay.

I would go on to grow with the organization, moving from supervision through varied management and executive positions. Bryan Memorial Hospital morphed into Bryan Health, a well-respected regional cardiovascular referral center in the Midwest.

I will always remain indebted to the director (and the organization) for taking a chance on me and providing me this opportunity at a young age so early in my career. I never miss an opportunity to speak fondly on behalf of this organization.

They ignited a fire *within* me that would burn for another twenty-plus years at Bryan Memorial Hospital prior to my first CEO position. Back then, we did not speak of becoming inspired or inspiring others; nevertheless, I recognized, felt, and believed in the *symptoms*. I committed to spreading the *disease* throughout our portion of the organization as quickly and effectively as possible.

These were wonderful years, marked with tremendous horizontal and vertical growth. The areas I was ultimately responsible for included most of the ancillary service lines. Many of the new emerging technologies landed in these areas. The combined number of employees grew from approximately 10 to over 145 in just a few years. Forty of these individuals were highly specialized registered nurses, all of whom were employed outside of nursing services.

The point of all of this is (1) I was inspired *(the Spark)* to change the organization; (2) I played a role in inspiring others *(the Flame)* to change the culture throughout a significant portion of the organization; and (3) collectively, we inspired a small portion of the world *(the Torch)* by contributing to Bryan Health becoming a renowned regional cardiovascular referral center.

I have recognized *myself* in many young individuals throughout my career. My experience reminds me how important it is to be an inspiring, loving, servant leader who encourages, supports, and believes in those determined to make a positive difference in the lives of others.

3) Pain of Doing the Right Thing

Approximately two months into my six-month trial period, I faced a challenging situation, which created personal consternation and pain but provided lifelong conviction to making the right, but often difficult decisions.

I am thankful I prepared and presented the proposal, as described above. This chain of events, with positive outcomes, was instrumental in providing future opportunities and choices—all of which plotted the course for my professional career. Would I have done it again knowing the outcome? Absolutely.

As I reflect on it now, I better understand the challenges I faced at the time in seizing these supervisory responsibilities. These are some of the circumstantial realities:

1) I did not have previous formal supervisory experience. *Several in the department did have such experience.*

2) I did not have previous experience in respiratory therapy or any other clinical area of expertise. *Several in the department did have such experience.*

3) I had only been in my position for six months when I presented the proposal. *Most everyone had worked there longer than me.*

4) I had established friendships with most everyone in the

department. *I had placed emphasis on being friendly and working well with everyone.*

5) I was only a college sophomore at the age of nineteen years, hardly a seasoned academic or professional. *Several were older than me. Two individuals were in their late twenties.*

6) The other staff members were not aware of the proposal details; however, I had established myself as the one to *inspire* the department to new and higher levels. The pressure was on me to perform. But, because I believed God had positioned me there for a purpose, I believed in myself; therefore, I was determined to be successful in orchestrating positive outcomes.

After conducting department meetings to review operational expectations; modeling a varied, flexible twenty-four-hour a day, seven days per week schedule; and appearing unannounced at all hours of the night and day, I sensed operations were improving. Everyone appeared to be accepting my new role and adjusting to the new expectations.

By the end of week seven, I was feeling pretty good about how operations were progressing. It was just a little after 12:00 A.M. on a Saturday night of that week when I received a call from the nursing house supervisor at the hospital. After apologizing for the late hour of the telephone call, she proceeded to tell me the night respiratory therapist had reported to work in a drunken stupor. She was certain I should know—and confident I would want to know.

We only staffed one therapist on the night shift. Robert was the therapist in question. He was a likable guy, funny, and considered a reputable therapist. He was a premed student at the University of Nebraska. He and I had gotten along well and worked well together. He was an easygoing guy who could generally place a positive spin on most anything.

Within twenty minutes, I was dressed and on my way to the hospital. During the drive, I was preparing for what I needed to do. By the time I arrived at the Hospital, I was confident in my plan.

I confronted Robert in the department, at which time he was feebly attempting to prepare for the shift. It was obvious he was in no condition to be anywhere other than his own bed. The smell of alcohol was so strong, it permeated the air within the room.

After being assured of his safety in having a ride home, I told him I was not only releasing him for the night, but I was terminating his employment immediately. I worked his shift rather than drawing attention to the situation at that hour of the night. This was a most difficult decision for me.

Testing for alcohol consumption in the workplace was not a hospital policy at the time; but Robert's condition was obvious and corroborated by the nursing house supervisor and one registered nurse. To this day, I believe this is one of those egregious infractions that leaves one with little choice.

A couple of weeks later, Robert stopped by the hospital to visit with me. I was gratified when he told me he did not harbor any hard feelings, as he understood what he had done was irresponsible, inappropriate, and an endangerment to our patients. He also referred to it as a personal wakeup call.

I am pleased Robert went on to become a board-certified family physician and establish a reputable practice. Even though this was a most difficult decision, I look back on this as being the right thing to do, given the gravity of the circumstances.

This scenario was instrumental in crafting my conviction to be an inspiring, loving, servant leader—and to be as inspirational and supportive of staff as possible. Coupled with this is my personal belief we should exhaust all possibilities of training; orientation; education; leading through inspiring, loving, servant leadership; and adhering to the Golden Rule—treating others as we want to be treated.

FANNING THE FLAME... INSPIRE OTHERS

This chapter includes thirty-two practical suggestions and recommendations designed to help you utilize everything that has inspired you, as discussed within *The Spark,* to now inspire those around you—specifically, those you will depend upon to inspire the entire organization.

These developments are best described as a matrix relationship; rather than a linear relationship, with focus on:

(a) The Board of Directors
(b) The Leadership Team
(c) Other Directors, Managers, Supervisors
(d) Key Staff Members
(e) All Staff Throughout the Organization

In the previous chapter, entitled "Igniting the Spark . . . *Inspire Self,*" we focused on personal attributes for everyone in our intended audience, which includes, (1) CEOs, (2) leadership team members, (3) management staff, (4) individuals who are aspiring to leadership roles at all levels, (5) existing staff who want to contribute to a more inspirational culture, and (6) individuals who are seeking employment in high performing, inspirational organizations. All of the items (attributes, characteristics, and behaviors) we've discussed apply universally to everyone identified in the previous section.

Much of what was discussed was focused primarily on the CEO and others in leadership roles, but because we are human beings first and foremost, all of this is applicable to *everyone*, particularly to those listed as our intended audience.

In this chapter entitled, "The Flame . . . Inspire Others," the intended audience remains the same. I will transition from focusing on recommended personal attributes the CEO and other leaders should personally adopt to how they, in turn, can and should inspire, love, and serve others.

Not to be associated with trickle-down economics, I describe this process as *trickle-down inspiring, loving, servant leadership*. It should first be believed, adopted, presented, and modeled by the CEO and other members of the leadership team. From there, it should permeate and positively affect all others in leadership roles (directors, managers, supervisors), followed by all staff members within the organization. Thus, the name of this process: *trickle-down inspiring, loving, servant leadership*.

We have established that we are capable of *inspiring* one another, *loving* one another, *serving* one another, and *leading* one another, whether formally or informally. It is a matter of granting ourselves permission to be *more* of these attributes and modeling those attributes consistently at home and at work. I believe we become what we think about, talk about, dream about, and profess to be important.

Leaders, it is your responsibility to initiate and insist on these processes. I believe this is your most important responsibility and you must hold yourself accountable and you must be held accountable by others. If you master this effectively, I contend everything else will ultimately take care of itself.

1) **Board of Directors as Customers**

I believe it is fitting to begin with your organization's board of directors. At this time, I am speaking primarily to leadership teams, and more specifically, to CEOs. The composition, selection processes, and size of boards will vary with the type of organization, *i.e.*, governmental entity versus non-profit versus for-profit boards. Most of what I will share will be universally applicable to all three types. Admittedly, all of my experiences with boards of directors have been with non-profit entities, in my case, hospitals. I have also served as a board member on several other non-profit boards of directors.

After a significant number of years in working with various hospital boards, I have come to adhere to two basic principles: *First*, behind every *successful* healthcare (or any other) organization is an engaged and visionary board of directors; and *Second*, at the center of every *successful* board of directors is a board president who leads with a gentle and compassionate heart yet guides with a firm and deliberate hand.

Even though titles like Chairman, Chairperson, Chair, or President may be used interchangeably to describe the board's leadership role, I will refer to the position as president of the board.

You may be surprised I've entitled this section, "Board of Directors as Customers." In many smaller organizations, the board of director positions are voluntary, unpaid positions. I am often amazed by how much time some board members contribute on a voluntary basis. In a sense, all of us are customers of one another. In smaller communities, the board members and their families are most likely customers of the organization.

We need to invest in our board members by facilitating comprehensive orientation and training, providing ongoing education, keeping them informed in a timely fashion, and sharing and being accountable for the "less desirable" news, along with the good news. We should always remember board members individually, and the entire board collectively, assume fiduciary responsibility for the organization. It is administration's responsibility to ensure the board is well-oriented to operations, aware of upcoming changes in the organization's external environment, sensitive to present and future community needs, and has all the needed information for the board to make the best decisions on behalf of the organization in a timely fashion.

Early in my relationship with boards, and organizations in general, I committed that *I (we) would never do or support anything illegal, unethical, or immoral.* This was an ongoing commitment and standard that proved beneficial in establishing a respectful relationship with the board. It is good to reference this from time to time.

Figuratively speaking, it is important to never get out ahead of the board, or to get crossways with the board, and to avoid surprises at all costs. I suggest adopting a thirty-day notice commitment to the board, though there will be times when this may not be possible. Assuming most boards meet monthly, it is good to provide preliminary information at one meeting with plans to finalize decisions at the next meeting or at a subsequent meeting as determined. The primary objective is to never have the board feel they have been influenced into a forced decision, particularly without having all necessary information. Another advantage of the thirty-day notice policy comes into play when one or more board members are absent from one meeting, they will likely be exposed to the needed information at a second meeting, when they will be called upon to make a decision.

It is important to communicate with the board between meetings as may be necessary and appropriate. In an effort to keep the board informed before pertinent information becomes public, it may be necessary to email these updates directly to the board members. Such a decision should be jointly made by the president and CEO in most cases. Circumstances may dictate that selected transmittals be authored and signed by both the president and the CEO.

I recommend boards devote most of their time to these four critical areas: the organization's dream/values, quality performance improvement, new and embellished services, and financials. I am not recommending any particular order; though I feel strongly that more time and attention should be paid to quality performance improvement and less to financials. Traditionally, boards have focused their time primarily on the financial aspects.

In order to complement standing agenda items and reports at the board meetings, I suggest the CEO edit and prepare a written report, highlighting day-to-day operations. This should be included in the distribution of the board packet several days in advance of the board meeting. These highlights will most likely include items that will not be addressed in other standing agenda items and reports. I suggest staff, department directors, and leadership team members author these report segments and submit them to the CEO. The CEO can assume responsibility for editing these reports for accuracy and standard format. Format can vary, but I personally like the report to mimic newspaper headlines, followed by succinct information. It is important to also credit the authors of the various report segments, as this conveys a spirit of respect, contribution, and ownership.

I encourage staff to view this as an opportunity to communicate directly with the board, sharing information and accomplishments the board would not become aware of on a monthly basis. After the board meeting, I recommend distributing this report to the entire staff by personal email and including it on the organization's internal intranet. Distributed in this way, this report serves several purposes. This is helpful in keeping the organization informed, in recognizing individuals and departments, and honoring those who have contributed to the board report.

I promised to discuss the importance of the president of the board and the working relationship between the president and the CEO. A strong, mutually respectful relationship between the president and the CEO is of utmost importance as the board will take strength, direction, and confidence from such a relationship, often even deferring to the president and CEO for recommendations.

The president and CEO should visit frequently between meetings on an ongoing basis in order to reinforce this relationship. The CEO should ensure the president is always the first to know of timely and important information, before such information becomes public within and/or outside of the organization. In doing so, the CEO will not only honor the president, but encourage the president to do the same if he/she becomes aware of sensitive information.

The CEO should take every reasonable opportunity to invite the president to various meetings with outside organizations. Such involvement will strengthen the relationship between the president and CEO and prove helpful in moving initiatives forward in a timely and effective manner.

In order to model this relationship, I even suggest that the president and the CEO sit together at the board meetings. Furthermore, it is important for some elements of this relationship to be cultivated with and extended to the leadership team. I also recommend that the entire leadership team attend the board meetings and participate in presentations and discussions.

Such a respectful relationship between the president and CEO also emphasizes, models, and affirms separation of the primary roles of governance by the board and operations by the CEO and leadership team, and defines how the two operatives can exist in a mutually respectful and effective relationship.

It is also important to publicly credit and thank the board as often as possible for their unselfish service to the organization and thus, to the community. Such opportunities include board meetings, department director meetings, staff meetings, celebrations, community gatherings, and interactions with civic organizations.

It is very important to create an inspirational environment for the board of directors. I am reminded of the adage, *What goes around, comes around.* My experience has been just that, as the board and president of the board become inspired; they, in turn, provide inspiration back to the CEO, the rest of the leadership team, and the organization in general.

I have had the pleasure of working with a number of commendable board presidents, and I want to tell you about one of these relationships that stands shoulders above the others. Mr. Robert (Bob) Jackson has served as a trustee for a total of ten years and as board president for the last eight years. In his role as board president, Bob and I worked together for almost five years.

From the beginning, Bob and I seemed to just hit it off. We both experienced rather humble beginnings growing up on farms in the Midwest during the same era and having shared many of the same experiences. Bob was born and raised in a farming community in Missouri, served his country in the Navy, spent his professional life in California, retired, and moved back to Missouri. It was here he was tapped to become a trustee and ultimately the board president.

Working directly with Bob Jackson has been a real blessing to me both personally and professionally. Bob's thirty-nine-plus years of experience in business and manufacturing productivity, process improvement, finance, computer technology, and administration proved invaluable to our operations. His knowledge and experiences in these areas have not only proven to be transferable to healthcare but to be most enriching in our day-to-day operations. Bob and I shared, employed, and enjoyed the characteristics of the desired mutually respectful relationship described above. In the time we have known each other and worked together, we have never had disparaging words between us.

Bob gives of his time and talents in his roles as servant leader, mentor, teacher, confidant, consultant, and lifelong learner. All of his remarkable accomplishments and personal qualities have served him well as board president.

I am pleased to inform you Bob Jackson was nominated, selected, and honored as the 2018 Hospital Trustee of the Year by the Missouri Hospital Association. Bob is most worthy of this recognition—and it is my pleasure to honor and introduce him as such. In conclusion, I share I am a better person having known and worked side-by-side with Bob Jackson.

2) Establish a Balanced Leadership Team

This discussion will focus on the role of the CEO in selecting, establishing, and developing a well-balanced leadership team. Your leadership team should be both position- and strength-balanced. Assembling a well-balanced, effective leadership team will prove to be one of the most important series of decisions a CEO will make within the organization he/she represents. The leadership team, including yourself, will be the team you will come to rely on most heavily.

As the CEO, you will either be newly appointed to your role with a new organization, or you are currently in your role as CEO where you have been for a period of time. The dynamics may be similar in both circumstances, yet they will be unique to the organization.

If you are new to the organization, you will likely inherit some semblance of a leadership team. This will be the first group you should present (and model) yourself to as the inspiring, loving, servant leader you either are—or as the servant leader you are aspiring to become posthaste.

I recommend not making any additions or changes in the composition of the team until you have had an opportunity to become intimately familiar with existing operations. I suggest your first few weeks be dedicated to *one-on-one* visits with current leadership team members, department directors, managers, and supervisors, as well as with key staff members and as many staff members as possible. In order to expedite the process, you may want to meet with staff in department meetings, *with the department heads and other managers present.* I offer this as a cautionary note, as sensitivity to the human implications of such meetings across managerial levels can be critical to the leader's relationship with mid-level supervisory or managerial personnel.

No matter how you've arrived in your position as CEO, I recommend you start meeting immediately with the leadership team frequently, regularly, and as needed. During these meetings you will jump-start organizational learnings, accomplish needed and timely functions, become more familiar with the team members, begin assessing their individual leadership philosophies and abilities and evaluating what you need in team membership, assessing how well they work together as a team, observing other group dynamics, and talking about and modeling *inspiring, loving, servant leadership.* It is most appropriate and essential to seek the team's input regarding the size and needed representation of the team.

Everyone deserves at least one opportunity to have a fresh start with you at the helm, but if you come to believe you need additional members or you need to replace one or more current members, I recommend initiation of these processes as soon as you are confident in moving forward. Postponement of needed changes, after a certain point in time, will only result in additional agony for you, the individual(s), and the organization. Even these less-desirable duties of the job can be accomplished through inspiring, loving, servant leadership.

If you have been the CEO of your present organization for some time, it is likely you have already implemented and accomplished these steps with the leadership team. It is imperative for you to be satisfied you have the needed representation and the right individuals on the leadership team. If you do not, I recommend moving forward with the needed adjustments.

Determining the appropriate number of members on the leadership team will need to be based on the vertical and horizontal responsibilities of each team member and the size, growth strategy, regulatory requirements, and nature of the organization.

In a medium-sized hospital, for example, I would recommend that you have a leadership team consisting of the Chief Medical Officer (CMO), the Chief Nursing Officer (CNO), the Chief Operations Officer (COO), the Chief Financial Officer (CFO), the Chief Information Officer (CIO), the Chief Human Resources Officer (CHRO), and the Chief Executive Officer (CEO). This roster assumes a significant potential growth strategy, resulting in additional horizontal/vertical growth.

In order to grow effectively, it is important to have the correct organizational structure in place, especially as it relates to the leadership team. These are the individuals you will rely on to keep the organization as responsive and nimble as possible. These are key individuals who will join you in promoting inspiring, loving, servant leadership throughout the entire organization. Other managers will join the leadership team in this effort, but your team will be the catalyst in establishing the culture we are envisioning.

It is vitally important that each member of the leadership team believes in, subscribes to, promotes, and models inspiring, loving, servant leadership. I suggest you initiate team discussions and group consensus in support of these endeavors early. This is one requirement you should evaluate as your team becomes established. You need to be clear about this expectation. If this is lacking in any one or more individuals on your leadership team, I recommend you provide an appropriate amount of time with the naysayer(s) through one-on-one counseling with each individual privately. If it becomes apparent they will not be supportive of these philosophies, it is necessary for them to leave the team and seek another position within or outside of the organization, which provides better alignment. I am reminded of the comment I previously shared about Mr. Dale Johnson, one of my mentors, who used to say, "Go slow, so you can go fast."

3) Another Important Component of the Management Team

Thus far in this section, I have focused primarily on the CEO and the leadership team. I have referred to the CEO and the leadership team separately, but I consider the CEO a member of the leadership team. The leadership team is responsible for inspiring the overall direction of the organization.

When I refer to the organization's management team, I am including the CEO, the other members of the leadership team, directors, managers, and supervisors. I am all-inclusive when it comes to defining the management team. I want to emphasize the importance I place on the roles of these three management positions—the directors, managers, and supervisors. Of course, the titles and responsibilities of these positions will vary from organization to organization.

In addition to the leadership team, I find it *heartwarming* to consider everyone in these positions as being on one large management team. As a leadership team, individually and collectively, it is vital we profess and model inspiring, loving, servant leadership in a consuming manner, which engulfs all members of the management team with a sense of oneness— as inspiring, loving, servant leaders.

Directors, managers, and supervisors assume a great deal of responsibility as they couple day-to-day linkages between the leadership team and frontline staff. The onus is on the leadership team to instruct, equip, mentor, and model to the directors, managers, and supervisors what it looks like to be inspiring, loving, servant leaders. This a key role of the leadership team.

In turn, we on the leadership team look to the directors, managers, and supervisors to instruct, equip, mentor, and model to frontline staff what is looks like to be inspiring, loving, servants one to another and to those we have been called to serve. We ask directors, managers, and supervisors to carry a disproportionate share of the water in these endeavors; therefore, we as a leadership team must be inspirational, respectful, and supportive of their efforts in doing so. As one large management team, we *must* stand together—arm in arm—as we model inspiring, loving, servant leadership throughout the entire organization.

How do we bring everyone together as a management team so everyone feels valued, respected, supported, and appreciated? We could identify and discuss a variety of initiatives to achieve this end. An important measure is to demonstrate our respect, individually and collectively, for the directors, managers, and supervisors in how we communicate with them, how we energize them in seeking their ideas and recommendations, and how we include them in decision-making processes.

For example, if an announcement is being made to all employees, it is an important gesture to inform the directors, managers, and supervisors as a group, prior to informing all remaining employees. Depending on the nature of the announcement, this may be accomplished in a face-to-face meeting or conveyed by email to each individual. This is a common courtesy and reasonable expectation. Doing so says, "We value and respect you as a member of our management team," plus, it is inspiring and loving to do so.

I used the word *heartwarming* previously, when I referred to the one large management team. I will use it again as I describe our management team meetings, which I found personally *heartwarming*. I will share several recommendations regarding these meetings:

1) It is important to conduct management team meetings on a regular, monthly basis, with emphasis on making these meetings a high priority for all those on the attendance roster. This includes the CEO and the other members of the leadership team, as well as the directors, managers, and supervisors.

2) As the CEO, I prefer to lead and facilitate these meetings. It was my privilege to be in the presence of the entire management team, at least one time each month. Of course, there inevitably will be times when it is necessary to schedule impromptu meetings to communicate with the team in a timely and respectful manner.

3) I recommend creating an agenda for the meeting, distributing it in advance, and having hard copies available at the meeting. It is important for everyone to know they can recommend topics for the agenda, and to send the message this is *their* meeting.

4) There are three standing agenda items, which I (we) like to include at the beginning of each meeting. The first is *"Time of Reflection."* Members of the team volunteer to share the *"Reflection"* for the following meeting. The topic is to be inspirational and determined by the presenting individual. Generally, the presentation and discussion only lasts ten or fifteen minutes. This is inspirational, as we share together through a common experience, before turning to the business of the meeting. Often, members of the management team have been quick to volunteer.

Second, I *(we) provided a designated "Time of Recognition,"* as the second item on the agenda. The purpose is to provide opportunities for everyone present to recognize and thank individuals, groups, and departments throughout the organization, as well as community members for going *above and beyond.*

I generally conclude this period of time with this admonishment, "As you see these individuals out and about, please tell them we 'talked about them' in our meeting—and then tell them why." I have found these two activities set the tone and the mood for the rest of the meeting—and they bridge the time between our monthly meetings.

The *third* standing item, which can be placed anywhere on the agenda, is *"A Time of Sharing."* The process is simple: we go around the table from one individual to another, providing an opportunity for each to share information regarding new services, upcoming events, and other information within each of their respective departments. While it is important to provide everyone the opportunity to *pass*, as appropriate, this is an excellent time to share information with the group, seek specific feedback, and receive affirmation for their accomplishments—and to be inspiring, loving, servant leaders.

5) The seating arrangement for meetings in general, and for this meeting in particular, calls for seating around a large conference table or around a combination of several tables. It is my desire to have everyone seated around the table to adopt a spirit of *unity and equal representation.*

Sometimes, there will be one or more individuals who sit outside of the circle. This provides an excellent opportunity to tactfully remind everyone, *"We do not have any second chairs in our orchestra. We will need to draw the circle larger to include everyone."* To some, this may appear trite, but it conveys the message that each individual on our management team (and in other meetings) is equally important, regardless of position or title.

6) I often assure individuals that I am (we are) generally willing to openly share and discuss most everything that occurs within the organization, with the exception of confidential personnel information—providing individuals demonstrate willingness and ability to be respectful of the information and responsible as to how they utilize it. Appropriate timing is a determinant of when it may or may not be the right time to share such information.

A primary purpose of the monthly management team meeting is for the leadership team to openly share information, seek input, and engage the team in decision-making processes. We adopted a clear, tactful, and diplomatic approach in letting the management team know what is to be considered *confidential* within the team and what is not. Most everyone knows what *family business* is and what it *means*. We adopted this mantra to convey that specific information is to be considered *confidential* by the management team only—and is not to be shared at this time.

It is important to share information with the management team in a timely fashion, so they hear it first from the leadership team before learning about it from others. The time and effort invested in the management team is a good investment, assuring significant returns. Never miss the opportunity to affirm each member of the team as a valued member of the team and have them know how much they are appreciated. Through varying approaches and comments from one meeting to the next, this simple message of thanks is an excellent way to adjourn the meeting.

4) "InspirUnicate" Always; If Necessary, Use Words

The purpose of this segment is to discuss the importance of inspiring, loving, and serving others unconditionally, through a variety of modeling approaches and forms of communication. We are all inherently capable of modeling inspiring, loving, servant leadership. Since we are wired differently, we may find some forms of communication more appealing and effective than others. Some people prefer written communication, while others may be more comfortable with verbal communication.

I recommend that the leadership team, with the support of the management team, develop a slate of options for ensuring timely and effective communication across the entire organization. Given the number of social media formats available to us, this list of options has expanded greatly. We are reminded that these mechanisms are only *vehicles* to transport the message. The onus remains on each of us to communicate, or convey, the message in an inspiring, loving, and serving manner, regardless of the delivery method.

I have always appreciated this riveting admonishment by St. Francis of Assisi: "Preach the Gospel always, and if necessary, use words." Parallels can be drawn to our discussions regarding inspiring, loving, servant leadership. For this reason, I coined the word, *"InspirUnicate"* and the mantra, *"InspirUnicate always and, if necessary, use words."*

Our actions can certainly be more powerful than our words. *"InspirUnicate"* is a combination of the two words, *"Inspire"* and *"Communicate,"* with emphasis on the **"U"** for *You*—as in *"You Inspirnicate"* with and to others. I trust this harmless bit of wordplay may help *all* of *us* remember to always be inspiring, loving, servants with one another in what and how we speak—through our actions and our modeling.

It has often been said, *"We cannot overcommunicate."* I find more favor with this modification, *"We cannot overcommunicate inspirationally."* It is for your leadership team, with the involvement and support of the full management team, to determine the mechanisms most effective for your organization.

In the segment, "The Board of Directors as Customers," I shared how we had prepared and utilized the board report, not only as a tool to inform the board, but also as a communication back through the organization, crediting those who contributed to its content. In addition to monthly department meetings and management team meetings, other options may include quarterly all staff townhall meetings, open forums, morning huddles, coffee clatters, newsletters, or weekly and as-needed email updates, just to name a few. Regardless, of the mechanisms, the important thing is to "InspirUnicate *always and, if necessary, use words.*"

5) Making Decisions by Consensus

As a leadership team, I recommend the group agrees to make decisions on the basis of consensus, rather than by voting. This process may occasionally require additional time to arrive at a decision, but the extra time is worth the effort. Having to reach consensus often produces more insightful discussion and an appreciation for other viewpoints, all of which result in well-grounded decisions. I have found voting often becomes a divisive force in the face of efforts to create team unity.

Coupled with making decisions by consensus, I recommend the leadership team understands and agrees with this expectation:

> After a decision has been made, everyone will support and defend the decision, unconditionally, after everyone leaves the room.

As a buffer to the above two standards, I have found it helpful, as the CEO, to grant license to each member of the leadership team to reconvene the team if additional information becomes available, second thoughts or second *guesses* begin to surface, or other obstacles have been identified, which could alter the team's decision or course of action. Every member of the leadership team needs to know there is a safety-release valve. Let's remember, as discussed previously, *it is never too late to do the right thing.*

I also recommend the two standards discussed above be adopted throughout the organization as *our way of making and supporting final decisions.*

6) Pay Attention to Where You Park (Sit)

When meeting with another individual in your office, take a seat next to them (with appropriate distance between) on the same side of your desk and do not remain in your office chair with the desk between the two of you. Your desk and your high-back leather chair symbolize power and authority. The desk, by itself, symbolizes a barrier. These are not the messages you want to send as an inspiring, loving, servant leader. Taking a seat next to your visitor sends a message of *humbleness* and *"I am interested in our conversation,"* both of which are messages you intend to convey.

If you are meeting in a conference room, strive to sit on an adjoining corner of the table and suggest the other person take the head of the table. Once again, avoid having the individual sit across the table from you, as the table represents a barrier to your relationship and your interest in them as an individual.

In both of these imagined scenarios, I have implied the individuals are employees, which was my intent. In meeting with individuals from outside of the organization, I employ the *same* measures.

Your actions will convey your intended message. To complement your actions, use words if needed. If it is the first time meeting together, take the opportunity to tell your team members why you employ these gestures and why you are uncomfortable with traditional measures.

As the CEO new to the organization, I've recommended meeting first with the leadership team, and then with other managers, key individuals, and staff within the organization to become familiar with current operations, as soon as possible. I suggest employing these seating guidelines during these meetings, as these simple gestures will be immediately noted as you begin to model inspiring, loving, servant leadership. Actions *do* speak louder than words.

7) Surround Yourself/Organization with Specialists

One of the first pearls of wisdom I received early in my career was from Mr. Dave Olson, one of my mentors. He told me to "always surround myself with people who were smarter than me." (Perhaps, he believed this would be the only way I could ever become successful.) Over the years, I have modified this saying:

> Always surround yourself with people who have academic and experiential backgrounds, talents, skills, and interests different than your own—and be quick to credit them for their contributions.

While some may find this intimidating, I've identified it as a strength in character and a practice consistent with being an inspiring, loving, servant leader. It also becomes a built-in mechanism to keep me grounded, humble, and dependent on these individuals. In turn, these *specialists* become inspired to assume ownership, responsibility, and accountability for the positive changes they inspire in the lives of others—and throughout their operations. What goes around, comes around—and I find myself being inspired with their remarkable accomplishments.

Inspiring, loving, servant leaders are responsible for promoting inspirational work environments that encourage employees to be creative and to take risks. If we are to hit the bulls-eye, we need to tolerate (to the greatest extent possible) employees missing the mark occasionally. To summarize:

inspiring, creative work environments promote risk-taking, which leads to a sense of ownership, which transcends to striving to be responsible, which matures to becoming accountable as inspiring, loving servants.

These comments certainly pertain to the development of the leadership team and the other managers throughout the organization. More importantly, these same philosophies apply to everyone throughout the organization. We, as CEOs and other leaders, should view it as our responsibility to create an atmosphere, a culture, where *specialists* abound—and we should treat them accordingly.

8) Writing the Next Chapter

As CEOs and leadership teams, we are entrusted with significant responsibility in writing the *next chapter* in our organizations' history book. How do we want to be remembered? If we cannot leave a legacy for both, would you choose to be remembered as an inspiring, loving, servant leader—*or* for increasing revenue by 10 percent year-over-year under your tenure?

If you are successful in becoming known as an inspiring, loving, servant leader, you will likely be remembered for exceeding financial and other benchmarks year-over-year. It is amazing what an organization can accomplish when it is comprised of inspired employees who enjoy their work, love and care for one another, strive for quality performance improvement, yearn for learning, and enjoy working together, trying new things, and being gratified with work well-done.

These are the basic requirements for the success of an inspirational book: one or more authors; inspiring characters, subject matter, narrative to draw us in, illustrations to embellish the narrative, and an editor and verbalization that is effective in promoting the storyline, as illustrated below:

<u>*Book Requirements: Your Chapter in Your Organization's Book*</u>

Author(s):   Inspiring, Loving, Servant Leaders
Characters: Highly Inspired Staff—*not* Highly Motivated
Subject matter: Employee and Organizational Dreams
Narrative: Organization's Inspired Story
Illustrations: Upside-Down Organizational Charts
Editors, Readers: Perceptions and Opinions
Promotion: Verbal Repetition in Sharing Our Story

Most of us have an inherent need to make positive differences in the lives of others and a desire to leave this world a little better than we found it. Leaving a legacy is not just reserved for the rich, the famous, or public servants in high places. We will all leave a legacy behind for future generations. It is our choice to determine the nature of our legacy—and how we want to be remembered—both personally and professionally.

It is never too late to do the right thing and rewrite our chapter(s), our legacies. How do you and your leadership team want to be remembered—on and off of the field?

Mr. John Henry (Jack) Zohner, a local successful businessman and writer who contributed to our daily newspaper regularly for almost twenty years, recently announced his retirement. The newspaper, and the staff of his company, teamed-up and sponsored this large-print, half-page tribute to Mr. Zohner:

Thank you, John Henry (Jack) Zohner, for the last 19+ years of educating all of us, while saving lives with your articles. You truly are an inspiration to all of us! Jack said it best: "If your job is your passion, it is more of a hobby than a job. You will have no regrets. Never forget who you are, where you came from, who put you there, and where you are going . . . oh yeah, and the most important thing is while you are making a living, don't forget to have a great life!" Thank you for making us better people. Thank you for being our everyday hero.

What a commendable way to honor a positive difference-maker while he is still living. Jack is destined to leave an admirable legacy—for his family, his company, his employees, and the readers who faithfully followed his writings for nearly twenty years.

9) Upside-Down Organizational Chart

While you (the CEO) and the rest of the leadership team are determining the desired size, representation, and composition of the leadership team and management staff, it is a good time to focus on the illustrative value of this tool we affectionately refer to as the *organizational* chart.

I first became exposed to traditional organizational charts when I was still a college student employed by Bryan Memorial Hospital. We never had organizational charts back on the farm, so I found these intriguing, somewhat overwhelming, and a bit intimidating. I remember trying to find my position, as a respiratory therapist, on these charts. Finally, I realized my position was represented at the lowest end of the departmental leg on the chart—and I remembered thinking, *"Maybe my job is not as important as I had been led to believe."*

Some years later, as I was defining *my* leadership style and selecting tools for *my* management toolbox, I became determined to change the implied and inferred messages conveyed by the traditional organizational chart. I found these messages inconsistent with those of an inspiring, loving, servant culture and organization.

During these considerations, we decided to draw our organizational chart upside-down. As a hospital, this placed the patients at the top of the chart and the board of directors at the bottom, directly below the CEO. For ease of comparison with other industries, *patients* can easily and appropriately be substituted with *customers*.

It is not my purpose here to discuss all of the various types of organizational charts or to promote one particular type. We have generally utilized one chart for the entire organization, which we described as a functional chart. There are no names and no specific titles listed on the chart, other than the titles (only) of the leadership team. This arrangement places the names of the departments, which are listed from bottom-up in alphabetical order, above the respective members of the leadership team. The departments are listed in descending alphabetical order to connote that all departments are equally important.

Following is an example of an abbreviated functional organizational chart, with only four fictitious departments and two leadership team members, in addition to the CEO:

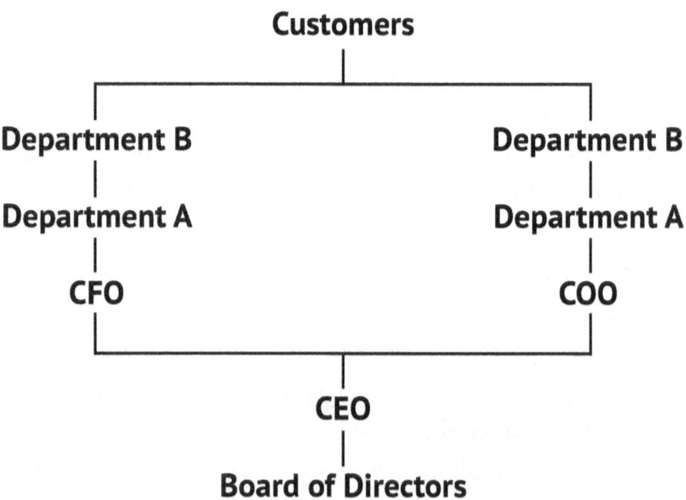

Following is a list of messages intended to be conveyed by the chart to staff and outside groups, as appropriate. I recommend utilizing this as a management tool. In appreciation of the old adage, *A picture is worth a thousand words,* I have added, *a thousand words can embellish the meaning of a valuable picture.* In addition to openly displaying the chart, it is important to describe and discuss these intended messages whenever possible:

1) This upside-down organizational chart connotes our commitment to inspiring, loving, servant leadership in the spirit and example of Jesus, who came to earth to serve and not be served. Everyone serves the positions (and the individuals represented) listed above their own position.
2) We are all here to serve the *customers,* those we have been called to serve. The customers are listed at the very top of the chart to represent our commitment to customer service.
3) The board of directors, having fiduciary responsibility for the organization and also directly for the CEO, is listed at the bottom, serving the entire organization.
4) The CEO is ultimately accountable for the entire organization and every staff member thereof.
5) This is what we have described as a functional organizational chart.
6) None of the boxes include names or titles. The leadership team boxes include titles, but no names, for the purpose of displaying departmental alignment within the organization.
7) The leadership team exists for the purpose of serving those not only within their individual departmental legs of responsibility, but the entire team; they collectively serve everyone above the team.
8) Departments are identified by name and listed alphabetically in descending order from bottom to top. This is to emphasize that all departments are of equal importance. Ordering the departments in this fashion dissipates any concern about one department being more important than another.

9) It should be noted that each department has some level of management included in the box, which is not identified. It is understood each department director, manager, or supervisor serves those within their department—and collectively, everyone above.

10) Departments are encouraged to have organizational charts representing their operations. If they so choose, we do ask that these charts be prepared in the same upside-down fashion.

This organizational chart conveys a powerful statement and commitment regarding our style of inspiring, loving, servant leadership. It is absolutely necessary that each leadership team member subscribes to servant leadership as connoted in the organizational chart. It is also important that each member promotes the chart and the underlying implications of its organization.

Finally, it is crucial that each member of the leadership team consistently models inspiring, loving, servant leadership. *Profession* and *Practice* must be congruent and in total alignment. If not, organizational credibility will begin to crumble at the foundational level and the crumbling will quickly gravitate upwards.

Though not anticipated, the first day of my first CEO job provided two early opportunities to model inspiring, loving, servant leadership that I will never forget. Remember, I am the one who likes to say, "There is always a little good in what appears to be the worst at the time."

The interview process I conducted with the leadership team over a period of several weeks had been quite intense. During this time, I had met and interacted with the existing leadership team, many of the department directors, other managers, the staff, and the physicians. I had prepared well for the interview process. I'd memorized the names of the leadership team, directors, managers, supervisors, and key staff members, *i.e.,* physicians, so I could address them by name, often before having actually been introduced. This preparation would serve me well during this first day.

As I had done with each director during the interview process, I had spent individual time with Joe, the director of plant operations. Considering myself a good judge of character, I had cast Joe as a friendly, likeable, competent guy who had witnessed (and survived) many changes at the facility. He had weathered the tenure of several CEOs and appeared to be the go-to guy for all issues related to buildings, equipment, maintenance, and the campus in general. He also struck me as a bit of a pleaser—but, aren't we all from time to time.

I was pumped for my first day. I remember arriving at my new office about 7:00 A.M., hoping to get a jump on the day. As I have for many years, I parked in the far corner of the back lot behind the facility. About 7:15 A.M., Joe stopped by my office. After brief exchanges of small talk, Joe asked, "Where did you park this morning?" Then he proceeded to tell me he had installed a reserved parking sign with **Mr. Steinkruger, CEO** printed on it—right outside the front entrance to the facility. He was so pleased with himself—and he was even more pleased with this attempt to please me.

I started to speak and then, I paused. In an instant (even though it felt like a minute), God prompted me with this caution I learned from my grandfather: *"Remember, have expectations, but never break the spirit,"* as I had relayed in the opening chapter. How was I going to turn this into a teaching moment—without breaking Joe's spirit?

I asked Joe to have a seat at the head of the small conference table in my office and I sat on the adjoining corner. I proceeded to tell him how grateful I was for his respect and thoughtfulness in preparing this *special* parking space for me. I told him I had been impressed with his knowledge and passion for his work at the facility, along with his historical perspectives of the operations, all of which, I would no doubt tap and find helpful in the future.

Next, I told him I appreciated this opportunity to address some personal perspectives. I shared my convictions regarding servant leadership and why I would not be comfortable parking in a special space, in such a prominent location. I told him about all of us being on the same team, just playing different positions, and that everyone's position was important—not just mine. I took the opportunity to tell Joe I was (and still am) an informal person and I granted him permission to refer to me as Rog or Roger—and certainly, *not* Mr. Steinkruger. He chuckled.

In response, he acknowledged and said he *liked my way of doing things.* He had personally prepared and installed the sign because every other CEO preceding me had been enamored with this special parking space. By 8:00 A.M., the sign had been removed. I never told another employee about it, and not many had seen it during its short duration, but this incident became common knowledge in a short period of time. I had conveyed a message to the entire staff, via this teaching moment with Joe. Regarding Joe's spirit, this incident jump-started our working relationship from day one. Truly, there was a little good in what appeared to be the worst at the time.

After Joe left my office, I returned to my desk to ponder the rest of my first day. By this time, it was a few minutes before 8:00 A.M. At approximately 8:05 A.M., my telephone rang, making this the first call I would receive as the new CEO: "Mr. Steinkruger, this is Barb at the front desk, I apologize for bothering you so early, but I wanted you to know the State Survey Team is here for an unannounced survey." (I did not take time to grant her permission to call me Rog or Roger, given the circumstances.) I told her I would be there to greet them momentarily. I immediately asked my administrative assistant to contact members of the leadership team to inform them, (1) the State Survey Team is in the facility, (2) I was greeting the Survey Team in the front lobby, and (3) to ask each leadership team member to join us in the main conference room as soon as possible. I had also asked my assistant to invite all other directors, managers, and supervisors to a meeting with the Survey Team at 9:00 A.M. in the same conference room. The leadership team was also made aware of this second meeting.

I will digress for a moment. After a previous recruiting effort lasting several months, a CEO had been chosen for the position—my position. This individual was to begin his duties within a couple of weeks at the time, when he notified the board that he would not be accepting the position. By this time, the position had been vacant for approximately six months.

To the credit of the board, upon the previous CEO's resignation, they had appointed five individuals to serve as the CEO transition team. As implied, this team had been functioning together for approximately six months when they found themselves needing to re-energize the CEO recruitment efforts for a second time. I was not a candidate during the first wave of recruitment; therefore, it was a blessing for me to learn of the position and join the new list of candidates. The second recruitment effort lasted almost another three months, leading up to this, my first day.

This was all openly explained to me when I interviewed on-campus. It was clear to me this team was functioning as a leadership team—at a high level, I must add. They all had at least five years with the organization. They appeared to be well-organized, had good organizational representation, worked well together, presented themselves as knowledgeable and confident, interacted well with the staff, and had fun working together as a team. I had noted this as an attractive feature in this CEO opportunity. By the time I had joined them on this

Monday—my first day—they had already been functioning as a leadership team for approximately nine months.

I was confident this team would be on top of the survey. These types of surveys were not new to the team or to me. In addition to State Surveys, the facility was Joint Commissioned Accredited, so this team had been through both types of surveys before, as I had also experienced over a number of years.

Back to the reality of the hour. I had consumed enough time with the Survey Team to allow all members of the leadership team to be in the conference room by the time we arrived. After completing introductions, and the Survey Team shared their opening remarks, it was our turn to speak.

I calmly began by thanking the Survey Team for gracing us with their presence, as we considered them to be on our team in delivering high-quality patient care. I assured them we would make all records, staff, and patients readily available to them during their visit. I explained this was my first day as the CEO of the organization and, of course, this prompted a few smiles and light laughter. In a serious tone, I assured everyone that, as the CEO, I assumed total responsibility for the survey, their findings, and any follow-up requirements.

I went on to explain to the Survey Team how this leadership team had been serving as the CEO transition team for over nine months. Going further, I explained how I had become acquainted with each member of the leadership team, and with each of them collectively, through the detailed interview process I'd followed. I went on to say how impressed I was with the leadership team's accomplishments during this transitional time and affirmed that I had total confidence in each of them individually and, again, with all of them collectively as the leadership team. This was all according to my purpose and my plan, which was being formulated by the minute.

We had concluded these exchanges a few minutes before 9:00 A.M. when the other managers joined us for the second meeting. I had told the Survey Team I would like to provide an abbreviated repeat of the first meeting with the exception that I open and facilitate this larger meeting. Once again, there was method in my madness. I was still looking for the *good* in what appeared to be the worst at the time.

At 9:00 A.M. sharp, we started the second meeting. I began by thanking everyone for their attendance on short notice. I introduced the Survey Team and made a special point of welcoming and referring to the Survey Team as members of our larger hospital team in providing high-quality patient care. I commented that our basic business is one of building collaborative relationships—even with surveyors. Then I proceeded to tell the managers, who had joined us, everything I had shared earlier with the Survey Team. This included my statement, as the CEO, that I would assume responsibility for the entire Survey process and outcomes and there would be *no blaming*. I also acknowledged my respect and appreciation for the CEO Transition Team's accomplishments during the last nine months.

Here is where the deviation occurred, as I then turned my attention to the directors, managers, and supervisors, I expressed my appreciation for and confidence in them as well, as members of the hospital management team. Before turning attention back to the Survey Team for their opening remarks and survey schedule, I thanked the entire hospital management team for the opportunity to join this fine team of hospital managers, physicians, and all the staff—and let them now that I considered it a privilege and blessing to do so.

The Survey Team concluded their remarks with appreciation and affirmation of the points I had intentionally shared in the presence of the Survey Team, the leadership team, and the other members of our management team—all on behalf of the organization. After a brief exchange of questions and answers, we adjourned the meeting and proceeded with the survey. We assured the entire management team that everyone would be invited back for the Survey Report-Out Meeting, to be scheduled by the Survey Team at the conclusion of the two to three-day survey.

It seemed as though everyone left the meeting walking a little taller with greater confidence than when they'd entered—including me. I was gratified I had found the good in what had appeared to be the worst, for a second time on this, my first day. Even though I was making it up as the day unfolded, I tallied these accomplishments for the day and the process:

1) I had been blessed with two opportunities to model inspiring, loving, servant leadership on my first day.
2) Even though this was my first day, I publicly announced I would be totally responsible for the survey process, the outcomes, and any required corrections. I also made it clear there would not be any blaming through these processes. (The inspiring, loving, servant leader accepts and acknowledges responsibility and does not assign blame—ever.)
3) I had been granted the opportunity to introduce and engage the Survey Team as *friends* and not *foes*—and model this to the management team. (As some of you know, this is not always the outcome of such surveys, as these can become adversarial in nature. I would learn later this had been a tendency during some previous surveys of our organization.)
4) I had recognized the fine work the CEO transition team (the leadership team) had accomplished, along with the confidence I personally placed in the team.
5) I had also recognized all of us (leadership team, directors, managers, and supervisors) as being on the management team and the confidence I had in this larger team.

6) I had involved all managers in the entire process, from start to finish. Everyone was able to hear everything said by the Survey Team. I later learned this may have been the first time this had occurred, as such events were generally reserved for the CEO and a few key individuals.

7) The individuals responsible for managing needed improvements were inspired and felt valued through the process of being included and hearing the entire survey story from start to finish.

Here's the rest of the story: The survey went well with only a few minor infractions; most of which were corrected before the team left the facility. The most notable outcomes were the positive and inspiring comments the Survey Team shared:

1) They felt welcomed and acknowledged for the purpose of their visit. They also added they had enjoyed being in the facility and had learned a great deal about our operations.

2) In addition to discussing noted infractions, they expanded their visit into an educational opportunity by complimenting staff for the good and notable processes in place, in addition to offering suggestions. They also honored the staff by seeking permission to share what they considered "best practices," with other organizations.

3) They commented on how open, relaxed, knowledgeable, and confident the staff appeared to be, along with their willingness to be of assistance throughout the process.

Years later, as I relay these experiences, I want to provide credit where credit is due; specifically, for the overall clinical outcomes of the survey. As such, I credit the extraordinary accomplishments of the CEO transition team (the leadership team) during the vacancy of the CEO.

10) Treat the Team Like a Team

When meeting with outside groups, agencies, and other organizations for the first time, include the entire leadership team and provide each team member an opportunity to be introduced and speak about their educational background, work experiences, and current responsibilities. The same courtesy should be afforded to representatives of the organization you are meeting with at the time. I've referenced first-time meetings, but including the entire team may also be appropriate during subsequent meetings with these same outside groups.

Over the years, I have developed a template for these types of meetings that has worked well. Generally, I facilitate the meeting and tailor the agenda to the nature of the group and the purpose for the meeting. I begin by extending a sincere *welcome* and expressing our appreciation for the meeting, and I then share some brief information about the organization: our story, our accomplishments, our dreams as an organization, and some of our operating philosophies. At this juncture, I would turn attention to the leadership team members collectively, and then to each member individually—always in a complimentary fashion. This is another suggested approach to building an inspiring, loving, servant leadership team. In doing so, you will accomplish these dynamics:

1) The representatives of the visiting organization will learn a great deal in hearing from all of us individually—and collectively. In turn, we will learn a great deal about them.

2) The manner in which we conduct the meeting will provide insight to our visitors in observing how we are structured and how well we work together as inspired, loving, servant leaders. It can also be viewed as an opportunity to model *hospitality*.

3) The leadership team will feel honored and inspired to

be included in these meetings, particularly if these are high-level meetings.

4) These meetings provide an opportunity for me to model my approach to such meetings in an informative and respectful setting. It also provides license for the leadership team members to share the same information in other settings they are facilitating.

5) These opportunities help solidify our knowledge of operations, they help us remain current on activities throughout the organization in a timely fashion, and are helpful in appreciating the big picture. This is beneficial in adding consistency to our messages.

6) These interactions provide yet another opportunity for the leadership team to demonstrate ownership and accountability for their portion of the organization—and for the organization as a whole.

7) It is good for the leadership team to hear about the backgrounds of their teammates. This an example where repetition from time to time is good.

8) Meetings provide opportunities to acknowledge, compliment, and honor one another by offering embellishments to the individual presentations.

9) Hearing the same information at the same time, may be helpful in finalizing strategic dream initiatives in a timely fashion.

10) It creates and maintains camaraderie among members of the leadership team performing as a high-functioning team and taking pride in their collective accomplishments.

11) Identify Key Initiatives

As the new CEO, or the CEO who has been in his/her position for a period of time, you have been focusing on the development of the leadership team. Presumably, you have also initiated the one-on-one interviews, not only with the leadership team members, but with directors, managers, supervisors, key staff members, and many frontline staff individually or through group meetings.

You have no doubt identified common themes regarding organizational strengths, weaknesses, needs, deficiencies, and proverbial problem areas. Discussing your list of findings will be a good exercise for you and the leadership team to focus on collectively.

After having completed the process outlined above at one of the hospitals I served as CEO, the leadership team tackled the list and established priorities. I want to discuss this process and our experience.

I met with representatives in the job categories I listed above over a period of approximately four weeks. As much as possible, it is good to gather the information and honor the individuals by meeting privately. You need to be prepared to hear about everything, most of which is on someone's list of needed improvements, regardless of how trivial it may appear to you. To the individual, it may be very important, so be patient in listening. It is important to remember these individual sessions provide opportunities to model inspiring, loving, servant leadership through your listening, seeking, and sharing. Be prepared to grasp the teaching moments.

In the midst of the deficiencies (and strengths) I had entertained, I identified three critical areas I heard about repeatedly. Not in rank order, these included, the need to (1) update, standardize, and promote all of the policies and procedures throughout the organization, (2) commit to and develop an enhanced quality performance improvement system throughout the entire organization, and (3) update and implement a well-designed and maintained electronic medical information system. To be clear, the facility had remnants of all three, so the challenge would be to take all three areas to a higher level.

The leadership team identified with these findings, and as a team, we agreed to embark on these three initiatives. One of the team members made the observation that all three initiatives were related to one another and our success in any one area would be reflected by our success in all three areas. In order to establish an enhanced quality performance improvement system, we needed up-to-date, standardized, easily-accessible policies and procedures in an electronic format.

Anticipating that the new focus in healthcare would be placed on clinical outcomes versus the number of delivered procedures, it was clear the quality performance improvement measures would be vital to all other healthcare operations. In turn, having an updated computerized medical records and information system would be crucial to capturing, measuring, and reporting the clinical outcomes. Since *every employee* in the organization would be positively affected by all three of these initiatives, it would be necessary to *inspire* all employees in the organization with a desire to be involved.

As the leadership team announces the priority initiatives to the entire staff, it is important to (1) review the process that led to the selection of the priority initiatives, (2) acknowledge and thank the staff for their input, which was instrumental in making these selections, (3) help the staff connect the dots as you describe the interconnectivity and importance of these initiatives, and (4) extend a sincere invitation to each staff member to become not only supportive of these endeavors but actively involved in designing and implementing the final products. The most important thing is to accomplish these four objectives through the words and passion of inspiring, loving, servant leaders.

I recommend embarking on one or more crucial initiatives that will improve overall organizational operations and involve every staff member. These initiatives become organization-centric. I am pleased to share the rest of the story. On behalf of the entire organization, within eighteen months we had not only mastered all three initiatives, but we had exceeded expectations in some areas:

1) We had subscribed to an electronic policy and procedure management system, which also was beneficial in developing new policies and procedures for the entire organization. Each of the approximate 1,500+ policies and procedures was reviewed. Policies were combined when appropriate, standardized in format, and loaded into a computerized production, editing, and retrieval system. We were able to reduce the number of policies and procedures by approximately 20 percent. This moved from being one of the most noted deficiencies to being referenced as an organizational accomplishment with great merit.

2) To demonstrate and document emphasis and outcomes regarding our quality performance improvement initiatives, we became DNV Accredited by a leading national healthcare accrediting organization. We were the first hospital in Missouri to attain this status. In joining DNV GL, we committed the hospital to having at least one unannounced survey each year. A few months later, the hospital was honored by achieving DNV's highest level of accreditations—ISO 9001.

3) We renewed the partnering relationship with the existing electronic medical records company based on the *one-team* concept previously discussed. As a result of this arm-in-arm relationship and mutual accomplishments, the hospital was asked to be one of sixty-five hospitals nationwide to serve on the company's National Advisory Council. Also, as a result of this highly-collaborative relationship, the hospital was afforded the opportunity to join an Accountable Care Organization (ACO). As discussed previously, *Good things do fall out of collaborative relationships.*

These are just a few examples of what can happen when employees are inspired to become more and do more, both personally and professionally. In addition to the gratification of employees working in a more inspiring and loving organization, the customer (in this case, the patient) ultimately benefits, as represented at the top of our upside-down organizational chart. As we have learned, when a movement reaches the 30 percent tipping point, it is difficult to stop the inertia, even if we wanted to do so.

Characteristics and Benefits of This Approach

1) Identification of organization-wide initiatives relate to *every* employee and to those we have been called to serve—our customers.

2) Initiatives such as these reaffirm the necessity of seeking input and counsel from those closest to the work.

3) Such initiatives provide opportunities to involve a large, cross-sectional number of employees as department- and/or organization-wide representatives. These present opportunities for a large portion of the staff to personally experience modeling of inspiring, loving, servant leadership—and to pass it on.

4) Through their involvement, employees assume a posture of ownership, responsibility, and ultimately, accountability.

5) Most of the organization-wide initiatives call for commitment to quality performance improvement processes, which should be in every organization's toolbox.

6) Never miss an opportunity to credit the individuals and groups of individuals for the accomplishments. I contributed little to these successes other than providing license to proceed, *pushing some out of the nest* (to force them to learn to fly on their own), securing needed resources, and modeling and promoting inspiring, loving, servant leadership.

7) Accomplishing such initiatives provides many opportunities for the organization to celebrate achievements, which is another way to recognize and honor those who have contributed to success. They will find this inspiring.

12) If I Could Only Choose One (Two-for-One)

In the previous section, I discussed three organizational-wide initiatives we tackled simultaneously. As I reflect on this, instead of becoming challenging at times, it could have become overwhelming for the organization. We chose to address all three simultaneously because, (1) we felt a need to expedite these measures in preparation for the future and to stay viable under changing market conditions, and (2) we recognized the relationships among the three and believed there would be efficiency and cost-saving advantages to launching all three within weeks of one another.

Your leadership team will need to decide what is best for your organization, based on your size, external conditions, internal capacity, available resources, promotional strategies, costs—and most of all, what is best for your customers.

If we could have chosen only one of these initiatives, it would have been the emphasis on quality performance improvement. Providing you have sufficiently prepared the organization as an inspiring, loving, servant leadership organization, this will be one initiative, (1) that everyone can appreciate, relate to, and embrace as being important on behalf of those you have been called to serve, (2) it is the *right* thing to do, and (3) if successfully implemented, it will drive development and/or refinement in other deficient areas—the other two in our scenario.

There is another distinct advantage for choosing quality performance improvement, as a foundational initiative. This generally relates to organizational planning, monitoring, and periodic reporting. This is possible through the combination of *Strategic Plans and Quality Performance Improvement Plans.*

In a subsequent segment, we will discuss the merits of *Dream Statements* versus Mission and Vision Statements. Mission and Vision Statements have been integrated with what we have traditionally known as strategic planning. I have been frustrated for much of my professional life with feeble, repetitive attempts to prepare and manage these two separate organizational reporting processes—strategic plans and quality performance improvement.

For many organizations, a significant amount of time and money has been invested in the development of both processes, only to be shelved and not utilized for the intended purposes. For those who do attempt to make these living documents, the complicity of preparing, maintaining, updating, and reporting also absorb significant time, effort, and money—and ultimately, these processes become overwhelming, often toppling under their own weight.

We successfully implemented a unique approach that combined these two processes (strategic plan and quality performance improvement plan) into one process, one document, and one reporting process tailored for all groups, beginning with specific work groups, hospital committees (safety and patient safety), management team meetings, the quality improvement council, medical staff, and ultimately, the board of directors and DNV Accreditation. Having only one reporting form for all of these groups was practical and efficient.

This approach simplified these two processes significantly, saving considerable time, effort, and money. Not only was this combined process easier to develop, maintain, update, and report, it became a *timely, living* document, which proved beneficial to our operations throughout the hospital. It was also instrumental during our budget preparation processes.

The first step is to develop a *Dream* for your organization, as defined through the associated *Dream/Values* statement. We utilized the *five pillars*—*People, Service, Quality, Growth, and Financial*—credited to Quint Studer, M.D., as the basic structure for our *Dream Plan.* One requirement was that everything identified within the five pillars supported the ultimate realization of the *Dream.* Within each of these pillars, we defined 2–3 short goals, followed by action steps, target dates, and the name of the leadership team member identified to shepherd the progress within the specific pillar. This worked well, as every performance improvement initiative also has a quality element.

In summary, I recommend you build your organization on a quality performance improvement platform under the auspices of inspiring, loving, servant leaders. Make quality improvement a part of everything you do and produce. This applies to every individual and all departments in the organization, not just those considered clinical or customer-based. Doing so, as an inspired culture, fosters a contagious spirit within the organization—a spirit of working together, making one another and the organization better and better, improving quality performance in processes and products, and experiencing vertical and horizontal growth throughout the service area.

If you are currently struggling with the efficacy of maintaining the Strategic Plan and the Quality Performance Improvement Plan separately, I encourage you to consider combining these two processes. Doing so, will amplify the importance of both functions because this document will become a living document that will be utilized by a number of groups. Departmental and organizational communications will be more consistent, delivered more frequently, and will prove more beneficial throughout the organization.

13) Your Past is Your Past; Learn From It and Move-on Quietly
Avoid talking about all of the good things you did at previous places you have worked, unless there is something to be learned and/or reinforced by example—or you have been

asked to share. We should all be proud of previous accomplishments, but we should also practice humility in doing so.

Most of us have had this experience when someone frequently talks about how he/she used to *do such and such at such and such* a place of employment. In my early days as a new supervisor, we had a staff person (Dennis) who consistently (it seemed more like constantly) spoke in these terms. As his supervisor, I had been contemplating how I might best address this with Dennis. It had clearly become wearing on other staff—and on me, frankly. I told myself, *"I will wait for the right moment to speak with Dennis."*

One day, I overheard Dennis and another employee having a one-sided conversation. Dennis was going on and on about how he used to do things at the *other place* and how much better it was there. When the first opportunity presented itself, the other employee said what most of us had been thinking, "Dennis, if things were so much better there and you did so many things to make it better, why did you leave? Maybe, you should consider going back." There was a pregnant silence, and I sensed the other employee had left the room.

This was the last time any of us heard Dennis speak of his previous enviable experiences. This uncomfortable issue had been taken care of, and I was off the hook. The other employee had not only impacted Dennis, he etched this in my mind to serve as a reminder to never personally repeat this offense. It is offensive to those proud of their organization and their personal and professional accomplishments. Many individuals have devoted their entire professional lives to their current employer—and this should be honored.

All of us, and particularly CEOs, should remain cognizant that our previous experiences are helpful in our new roles and we should privately draw upon and employ these to add value to our new position—and to our new organization. We should sprinkle these lightly and sparingly—and generally, only when asked or through third-person examples. Now is the time to focus on the good you will have found, the current state of affairs, and the greatest endeavor—the creation of an inspiring, loving, servant leader culture within your new organization.

14) Forget the Negative; Compliment the Positive

Everyone has a first day and a last day with every employer we will have worked with throughout our careers. As we join organizations, I advise CEOs, other leaders, and all staff to refrain from getting caught up in hearing and entertaining all of the shortcomings of the former CEO, other individual(s) you are replacing, and/or the organization.

Having to hear about these shortcomings is one thing; but entertaining, encouraging, or contributing to these discussions, is quite another. Doing so is not characteristic of the inspiring, loving, servant leader you aspire to be during your tenure. Even if the previous incumbent's history with the organization appears to have been turbulent, we should remember, the individual (1) likely had good intentions when they originally assumed their duties, (2) accomplished some good things while in their position, and (3) it is not for us to judge, as we were not present during these times. We should also be mindful that the manner in which we respond, will provide license to observers to make judgements about our well-intended purposes.

Predictably, some of this unassuming entrapment will occur. I suggest you develop a prepared one- or two-liner which is respectful, but clear in describing your position on the matter and is upbeat in portraying your optimism for the future. I suggest something along these lines: "I appreciate you sharing your observations from the past. However, I was not here, and it is not for me to make any judgements. My focus, along with all employees, will be on all of us working together to provide the very best services for those we have been called to serve."

As you hear about good things that occurred under previous administrations, I recommend you grasp the opportunity to acknowledge the accomplishment and compliment those who were responsible for its success. I have generally added something to this effect, "I am grateful for everyone who has served this organization in the past, as their accomplishments have made it possible for me to be here today, serving with this incredible team." Such an opportunity will serve as a positive testimony to your nature as an inspiring, loving, servant leader.

15) Can You Imagine?

As inspiring, loving, servant leaders, one of our primary responsibilities is to create a culture, an organization that taps the talent within the organization and puts it to work. When I speak of skills and talents, I am including educational backgrounds, past work experiences, professional memberships, mentorships, memberships in community organizations and community service organizations, volunteer experiences, experiences in religious organizations, interests, and hobbies.

I have spoken of this previously through the years, but I have never promoted a voluntary initiative, focused on taking an inventory of these skills and talents within an organization. I still believe this would be an interesting exercise, the results of which would be a staggering list. Can you imagine what this list would look like on behalf of an organization with 250 employees?

When we hire a new employee, we hire the total being, a composite of all their skills, talents, and experiences as referenced above. We do not hire just a portion of the individual. They come complete with all of their life skills, talents, and experiences: family, educational, work, trades, professional memberships, community service, volunteer, religious, special interest groups, and hobbies.

What we know and what we do not know. We know every organization has a large cache of these skills, talents, and experiences within its entire organization. We do not know how massive such an inventory would be. We do know there are existing organizations with a significant percentage of their staff just doing enough to get by every day—because they are working in uninspiring organizations. How many times have you heard something said to the effect, *"I just do what I am told to do, nothing more?"* The staff should not be faulted for this, as the responsibility lies at the feet of the organization, more specifically, with the leadership.

Can you imagine the power of a workforce unbridled and inspired to draw upon all of the skills, talents, and experiences the staff members have to offer? There are organizations that have mastered the implementation and ongoing enthusiasm for such a culture, undergirded with inspiring, loving, servant leadership. These are the places where you hear people say things like, *"I would do anything for this organization." "They value me first as an individual; and secondly, as an employee." "They want the best for me, while I am giving my best to them as an organization." "They care about me, about us." "I look forward to coming to work each day." "I feel like I am making a positive difference in the lives of others." "They care about our families. They work with me so I can attend family functions." "I have learned so much here—and about myself."*

16) Leader as Facilitator and Facilitator as Leader

Before further discussion, I want to discuss two underlying principles to remember from this section: *First,* we are all leaders, whether formal or informal; *second,* we are all facilitators, whether formal or informal in nature. Even if we are participating in a small group discussion over morning coffee, we will be facilitating discussion.

I tend to be a visual learner. This is a mental exercise I have utilized for different purposes throughout the years. Please join me in taking a few minutes to participate in my directions. I ask individuals or a group of individuals to close their eyes and visually reduce the physical size of your facility down to dollhouse size—the size that will comfortably sit on a table. I then ask the participants to peer through the windows around the facility, imagine what you might see, and listen-in on employee conversations.

We will focus primarily on the interactions of employees within your miniature facility, not necessarily the tasks they are performing. What do you see? Do you see employees in small meetings, in large meetings, employees walking up and down the halls, greeting one another, visiting in the hallways, or on the telephone? What do you like about what you see and hear? What do you not like? What are the expressions on their faces? Are they smiling and making direct eye contact? How do they generally treat one another—are they polite, considerate, and respectful?

Everyone can be a leader and a facilitator in these little vignettes I have asked you to create in your minds. Let's focus on the small and larger group meetings. When facilitating a meeting, it is important to ensure everyone has an opportunity to contribute, ask questions, make suggestions, and remain on task. Become an expert in reading nonverbal communication, so you become an even better leader and facilitator. Doesn't sound too much different from what we should expect in normal, respectful conversations, does it?

In speaking to the CEO, other members of the leadership team, and all managers, I recommend you make it a priority to hone and model these skills because meetings, regardless of size, need to be facilitated effectively to unleash talent and maximize the human talent quotient. Inspiring, effective meetings assure the best possible decisions, maximize buy-in, and equip the organization to be nimble in making decisions and implementing initiatives.

In an inspiring, loving, servant leadership culture, more employees are involved in decision-making, decisions are expedited, implementation is streamlined—and typically growth, higher production, and increased productivity occur, followed by improved financial benchmarks. It is quite amazing what can happen when all employees are pulling together in the same direction because they want to—and because it feels good.

I hope you are still peering into the windows of your little miniature facility. Now, I would like for you to envision two miniature facilities, one that subscribes to inspiring, loving, servant leadership and the other that does not. What are the differences you see? What do you like and desire to replicate? What do you see that you find distasteful and commit to improve?

17) Seek and You Will Find—and Defend

As the CEO, you will find yourself in a balancing act from time to time, as you strive to coach leadership team members as independent thinkers and doers on the one hand and team supporters and promoters on the other. You will find inspiring, loving, servant leadership is the key ingredient common to both conditions. Remembering to model and emulate the behaviors you expect is important. This needs to become a team sport.

Following are several independent and team behaviors which will serve leadership team members and other leaders, well. This is one grouping of related issues:

1) Run to and not away from problems, issues, challenges, and opportunities to make a positive difference in someone's life. *Be proactive and responsive.*

2) Always meet employee and customer issues head-on in an inspiring, loving, and serving manner. If an employee or a customer has been wronged, apologize, and find

restitution acceptable to both parties—as soon as possible. *Be fair and just.*

3) Build confidence throughout the organization. Help everyone in the organization, starting with the board of directors, come to believe in themselves, one another, and in the organization. *Be confident, but humble.*

4) Coach everyone in the organization to be a leader, a facilitator, and an ambassador. *Be an investor in human development.*

5) Seek the opinions of others before offering your own. If you share your opinions first, you risk shutdown from others. As a result, the most meaningful comment, suggestion, or solution may be sacrificed for another less effective. You also run the risk of having your own opinion altered beyond recognition. *Be open and receptive.*

6) As individuals, a leadership team, and an organization, be as compassionate to individuals and as ruthless on processes and systems as possible. Through the eyes of compassion, never avoid making the tough decisions. *Be compassionate.*

7) Encourage and welcome suggestions, proposals, ideas, and new approaches by all staff, regardless of position or rank. As shared previously, if this opportunity had not been granted to me early in my career, I likely would not be sharing this recommendation. My entire career would have taken a totally different direction. *Be encouraging.*

8) Commit to *never doing anything illegal, unethical, or immoral.* Mean it and recommit to it often—to the board of directors, the management staff, employees, collaborative partners, and outside organizations, as appropriate. It will help you maintain your edge and your integrity. *Be principled and of high standards and values.*

9) When addressing an issue, adopt an approach of *turning every stone over* before jumping to conclusions without considering every potential consideration. *Be thorough.*

10) Whenever possible, make decisions on the basis of sound data, rather than strictly on emotion. *Be objective.*
11) Create an atmosphere where specialists abound and treat them accordingly. *Be respectful of and dependent on others.*
12) Create an employee-centered and family-focused atmosphere, which encourages employee participation in family activities. It is also important to maintain a spirit of flexibility, to the extent possible. *Be supportive.*

It is important for the CEO, the leadership team, and all other managers to coach, preach, and practice these principles consistently, to be characterized as, *"This is the way they (we) do things around here. We know what to expect from this team." Be a team member and a team player.*

18) Create a Yearning for Learning

Most of us agree it is important to promote ourselves individually as lifelong learners and, collectively, as learning organizations. What does this really mean? Life itself is a day-to-day learning experience, so we really do not need to pretend. Our work experiences represent a significant portion of these lifelong learning experiences, which propel us forward from cradle to grave. Lifelong learning is a God-given, inherent need we have as human beings. I continue to take pride in saying, "Every day, I learn something new, which I know to be true."

When we speak of lifelong learning and learning organizations, we are generally describing the organization's commitment to equipping employees with the training and education they need to master their jobs. This is necessary and important in establishing new proficiencies and maintaining existing ones. These are tools we must provide to our employees to support them in doing their jobs. This is good for the organization—right?

It *is* good for the organization. I am describing something of a higher calling. Previously, we established that organizations hire the total individual, not just the portion needed to do their jobs. Under the guidance of inspiring, loving, servant leadership, inspiring organizations care for the total individual and not just the work-related portions. We want the best for our employees *outside of work* as well as *inside of work*, as the two are inseparable.

I have offered hints of discussions to come when I have referenced *personal and organizational dreams*. Most of this will wait for subsequent consideration. If we are sincerely interested in employees realizing their personal dreams, why would we not also want to encourage and support them in learning new things, even if they're peripheral to their work? I believe in the old adage, *What goes around, comes around.* In this case, *"What goes around to encourage employees in becoming better, comes around in making the organization better—happier employees, loyal employees, increased productivity, and improved financial benchmarks, to a name a few."*

You may be thinking, *"We cannot afford to do this for everyone—this is way too expensive."* Take note, I have not said anything about paying for anything. I have used the word encourage, which could equate to things like nudging employees to do something they have always had a desire to do, providing a flexible work schedule, approving time away, helping them cut through what may be viewed by them as red-tape, identifying and directing them to necessary resources, loosening tuition-reimbursement restrictions, bringing off-campus classes to campus, identifying and utilizing cost-free, online education, and yes, maybe even paying for something.

Most organizations, and many employees, are members of professional and network organizations that provide in-person and online education for free (as part of membership fees) or at significantly reduced rates. Staff education is often negotiated as a condition of closing a sale, with partnering vendors. These are excellent resources to tap.

There has never been a better time to encourage staff to dream and learn new things on a personal basis—and provide support beyond just plain encouragement. Having established this, I also need to urge individuals to be mindful that not everything available online is of a credible nature. As servant leaders, we can also be helpful in this regard.

What a great time to be an inspiring, loving, servant leader. As a leadership team, I suggest you discuss and decide what being a *learning organization* is going to mean to your team and your organization. I trust this descriptive term will take on new meaning and each of you will speak often and openly about this throughout the organization. *Your practicing must be consistent with your coaching and preaching.* I hope each of you and others in your organization, will experience great happiness and joy in witnessing employees mastering something they have always wanted to accomplish.

One last additional insight: When providing required work-related training, it is much easier and more gratifying (for the servant leader) to have employees seeing training as an *opportunity* to make themselves and their company better, rather than as *drudgery* and complaining about *one more thing to do* in uninspiring cultures. Seize the moment and the opportunity as an inspiring, loving, servant leader and coach.

19) Create a Fair and Just Culture

The creation of a *fair* and *just* culture is a topic for the leadership team to address and develop consensus around. If effectively developed, these concepts are more likely to be successful in cultures and organizations that hold themselves to standards synonymous with those found in inspiring, loving, servant leadership environments.

Here are several introductory observations regarding *fair* and *just* cultures, which are applicable for my purposes. *First,* the framework of a fair and just culture ensures balanced accountability for both individuals and the organization responsible for designing and improving systems in the workplace. Such a culture is inherent in a learning culture that is constantly improving and oriented to consumer safety.

We have discussed the virtues of always focusing first on our processes and systems, rather than arbitrarily assuming employee error. From my perspective, this is one of the rudimentary principles underlying fair and just cultures.

As a *second* consideration, the philosophy of a fair and just culture generally goes hand-in-hand with well-structured quality performance improvement processes.

Third, involving staff from across the organization in designing, implementing, and maintaining credible processes associated with a fair and just culture is an excellent measure in building employee buy-in and trust. Such trust can be difficult to attain when employees in many organizations have historically been subjected to punitive measures without consideration being given to system or process failures.

I share the following scenario of events, which when played out over a period of several months, speaks to each of the above considerations. This existed at the same organization where we selected and implemented the three initiatives previously discussed.

For several years prior to these initiatives being accomplished, the hospital had reviewed incident reports in what was considered a traditional manner. The abbreviation of this painstaking process included these steps: (1) an incident or an error would occur, (2) the individual, affected individual(s), or department would hopefully prepare a hardcopy incident report, (3) the incident report would then snake its way progressively through the hands of the department supervisor, the department director, and then the chief nursing officer (CNO), who would review it, seek clarification, and pursue action as necessary, (4) The CNO would summarize the nature of the reports, document any follow-up, and report the results to the Patient Safety Committee for review. This process often had a lifespan of two to three months. One of the underlying premises of this laborious process was the emphasis on employees self-reporting.

These were some of the fallacies and shortcomings of this process:

1) Even though constantly promoted, few employees were comfortable in self-reporting errors. The numbers were very low. One could surmise potentially threatening errors were going unnoticed and undocumented. Staff were fearful of retribution, based on historical and punitive outcomes. Trust levels were extremely low.

2) The process was laborious, time-consuming, and only allowed for retrospective, rather than real-time reviews. The case and the evidence would often become cold before anything constructive could be done to correct process issues or train-up staff, as necessary.

3) The process was top-down in design and practice with little staff buy-in, confidence, or trust. It was not serving its intended purpose of identifying any trending process or individual errors, learning from these, and providing additional training, all for the purpose of improving patient safety and reducing personal and organizational liability.

These prescriptive, well-designed and functional processes must be inherent in any approach to establishing effective quality performance improvement processes. This was also a requirement in our commitment to become DNV accredited. As such, we focused on this and other processes simultaneously.

We started visiting openly with staff about our commitment to a fair and just culture and the need to totally reconstruct our reporting system. To that end, we (1) sought staff involvement, (2) assured staff our initial focus would always be on our processes and systems and not punitive in nature, (3) decreased the review and reporting steps, and (4) involved front-line staff in designing and providing training and education, as prescribed.

We continued to emphasize self-reporting. Over a period of several months, the self-reporting numbers consistently increased and the number of errors and incidents also increased substantially. As odd it may sound, we were pleased to see this occur. We believed this meant staff were becoming more trusting of leadership and our revised processes. From a liability perspective, this was also important. It is one thing to have lurking liabilities, to not know about these, and therefore, to not be able to make improvements. It is quite another to identify errors in a timely fashion, take corrective action as needed, and avoid potential liability and litigation in the present—and the future.

There were other collateral benefits. Staff experiences travel quickly through small- to medium-sized organizations. Employees across the organization became more trusting and willing to participate in other process improvement initiatives.

These comments, provided anonymously, serve as an appropriate summary of this section: "A fair and just culture is a concept related to systems thinking which emphasizes that mistakes are generally a product of faulty organizational cultures, rather than solely brought about by the person or persons directly involved." In a fair and just culture, after the incident, the question asked is, "What went wrong?" rather than "Who caused the problem?" A fair and just culture is the opposite of a *blame* culture.

A fair and just culture helps create an environment where individuals not only feel free, but feel encouraged to report errors and help the organization learn from mistakes. This is in contrast to a blame culture where individual persons are disciplined, fired, or otherwise punished for making mistakes, but where the root causes leading to the error are not investigated and corrected.

20) Organization as a Strong Corporate Citizen

As the CEO and leadership team, it is important to inspire the entire organization to be a strong corporate citizen. In many communities, the organization you represent may be one of the largest, if not the largest company in your community or communities. In turn, many of your employees and their families are residents of the communities you serve and represent.

I introduce this initiative in this segment and section as it sends an important message to employees that you not only care about them, but you care about their families and the community or communities in which they live. Building and promoting the organization as a strong corporate citizen is an opportunity to collectively live and demonstrate inspiring, loving, servant leadership on a grander scale.

21) Speak Well of Other Organizations

In a broad sense, organizations are manifestations of individuals. This is logical, given individuals (as employees) collectively comprise and represent the organization. Therefore, we advocate organizations should emulate the behaviors we expect from individuals. When we are speaking of corporate cultures, we are essentially describing the personality of the organization, which mirrors the individual personalities and behaviors of the people who staff it.

Previously, we made the case that organizations and companies should be as compassionate as possible, just as we advocate for individuals being as compassionate as possible when addressing the needs and shortcomings of employees.

Most companies have what they consider competitors in their market space. No doubt, we all agree competition is good. As a leadership team, I encourage you to avoid speaking unkindly about other companies—competitors or not. To the contrary, when the opportunity presents, find something good or at least neutral to say about the other company.

I do not suggest you be patronizing in any way. However, speaking unkindly sends the same message to your employees and community we discussed as individuals previously. It does not endear a sense of trust or confidence in the eyes of employees or the public. It conveys a message similar to *"I wonder what they say about me, when I am not present?"* It is important to remember, particularly in smaller organizations and communities, it is 100 percent certain employees in your organization personally know or are related to employees in these other organizations. It is not good when you or your organization becomes a topic of conversation over Thanksgiving dinner. If it is to be, you should do everything you can to ensure such conversation is of a positive nature.

22) Develop a Distaste for Gossip; Always Speak the Truth

In drawing from my early days growing up on the farm, I remember my first exposure to the word *gossip*. I have spoken fondly of my paternal grandparents and, more specifically, have shared my love and admiration for my grandmother. Many of my early memories place me in her kitchen. Perhaps this had something to do with her being such a good cook and baker.

In one corner of the kitchen, mounted on the wall approximately five feet above the floor, was this wooden box with a protruding cord and several appendages. I would come to fondly recognize this as their first telephone on the farm. They shared that telephone on what was referred to as a party line with several other families in our little rural farming community. Each family was assigned a telephone number comprised of "short and long" rings. These "rings" were produced by a small crank, which in turn, rang the two bells.

Being a party-line, everyone would know when someone else was being called. The telephone etiquette of the day, called for no listening-in on one another's calls. How well do you suppose this actually worked in practice? An acquired skill by some was to be listening in on someone else's call without them knowing you were on the line.

This system did have one important feature. When someone had an emergency, they could provide one long ring, which would summon available neighbors for assistance. The availability of this feature must have provided a great degree of comfort throughout our rural community.

I remember sitting at my grandmother's table doing whatever I was doing at the time—probably eating cookies. She would be having what I considered normal telephone conversation of the day, when suddenly, she would start speaking in a different language—at least something I did not understand. I would later learn she was speaking in German.

From the fray of musing family conversations, I would come to learn this meant she and her friends were *gossiping*. So, whenever they started speaking in German, I knew they were talking about someone or something they did not want anyone else to hear—or understand. Initially, I naively assumed this was to protect my innocent ears—and maybe some of it was.

Given my admiration for my grandmother, I am certain this was her only little vice. We would often joke with her about this later in life, and in her humble manner, she would just smile and change the subject.

As I reflect on this experience, I conclude, (1) this was the first time I remember hearing about gossip, (2) even at this tender age of six or seven, I sensed this was not a good thing to do, (3) listening-in on the conversations of others struck me as being disrespectful, and (4) I remember overhearing about hurtful (and often, untruthful) things which were passed-on by those who listened-in. These observations have morphed into convictions through the years to the point that to this day I abhor gossip or any derivative of the word.

Gossip, is defined as "casual or unconstrained conversation or reports about other people, typically involving details that are not confirmed as being true." I believe gossip is one of the most disruptive, selfish, degrading, unproductive, destructive, and costly tendencies of the human condition, found both in our personal and professional lives. If you do not already believe and feel the same about gossip, I hope you will come to the same conclusions I have without suffering personal or professional loss because of this pernicious practice.

Encouraging and expecting all employees to refrain from gossiping is a good example of the call to all CEOs that the buck starts and stops with the CEO, with the expectation that all managers and staff fall in line immediately behind her/him. This will be an excellent conversation for the leadership team, with decisiveness confirmed through consensus and commitment.

First, each of us needs to believe gossip is unhealthy for the organization (and family); and second, we always need to be prepared and poised to teach, explain, and model our convictions. It is important for all of us to send this message by (1) not listening to, entertaining, or believing gossip, and (2) by not contributing to the gossip line. *Do not tolerate gossip at any level or to any degree throughout the entire organization.*

During these conversations with the leadership team, other managers, and the entire staff, it would be a missed opportunity to not address the antithesis of gossip—always *speaking the truth* in everything we do and say. The definition of truth is: "that which is true or in accordance with fact or reality." This should be presented and discussed throughout the entire organization. To provide the opportunity for repetition, and re-commitment every time it is repeated, you may want to consider developing a mantra, such as: *Gossip Never; Truth Always.* These are words consistent with inspiring, loving, servant leadership.

If you do not remember any of the specifics from above, I encourage *everyone* in the organization to conclude, (1) gossip is just plain wrong, (2) it is disrespectful and harmful, (3) gossip is not consistent with inspiring, loving, servant leadership, and (4) I (we) commit to eradicating it whenever and wherever possible. This is also a good time to remind all that everyone in the organization is a leader.

23) Fewer Is Better

When it comes to resolving personnel issues, there are four things I know or believe to be true.

First, even if your organization's culture is exemplary in being held up as the model to all as an inspiring, loving, servant leadership culture, I can provide assurance you will still need to address personnel issues.

Second, even though I do not support this with research, I believe cultures comprised of inspiring, loving, servant leaders (all employees), will have fewer personnel issues to resolve per employee capita, than cultures not characterized as such. Inspired employees tend to be happier, more tolerant and loving, and enjoy working together and serving one another. As a result, such employees are more apt to resolve issues *under the radar* and ward off problems before they arise to significant and/or reportable levels.

Third, I found it important to always strive to resolve personnel issues at the lowest level possible, with the minimum number of individuals. Depending on the severity of the accusation, everyone is entitled to at least one opportunity to right a wrong. If this opportunity has not been afforded to the presumed violating party, inspiring, loving, servant leaders should redirect staff back to approaching the individual in a one-to-one, private setting.

In doing so, it is important to create a teaching moment and offer suggestions for handling the situation with a positive outcome in mind. A mild dose of role-playing may be appropriate. It is also appropriate for the leader to extend an invitation to the individual to report back and let the leader know if (or how) resolution was accomplished. This approach keeps the door cracked open, so the employee does not feel abandoned and provides reassurance the leader really cares.

Minimizing the number of individuals directly involved also reduces the number of bystanders, who by no choice of their own are placed in a situation where they subconsciously or consciously are deciding who is right and who is wrong, generally without having all of the facts. They may even be made to feel they must support one party or the other. This is not only unfair; it expends unnecessary energy and emotion.

Fourth, do not hesitate to involve human resources and/or external agencies (i.e., outside legal counsel) earlier rather than later if you sense the situation may be at risk of spinning out of control. If nothing else, provide a brief heads-up, so they are not caught off-guard at a later time.

Early in my career, I was certain I could handle an incident on my own. Further developments started happening at warp speed, and I found myself quickly in over my head. I decided to seek assistance from human resources. The human resources director blessed me with two favors that day: *First*, he provided much-needed counsel and direction, regarding the situation and the resolution thereof; and *second*, he provided an admonishment to me that I am now sharing with you in a gentler manner, as a recommendation.

His wise counsel has remained with me from that day forward, and now I share it with you. Even though I do not recall him using these exact words, "When the alligators start biting at your 'behind,' it is probably too late to consider draining the swamp"—or something similar to this, as I recall.

24) Fewer Policies is a Promising Sign

Every organization needs to create and maintain certain policies for specific reasons, e.g., meeting governmental requirements. It is not my purpose to delineate a list of such policies or the reasons why your organization should (or needs to) maintain them. It is my purpose to convince you that fewer policies are better than many. In most organizations, we have become policy-happy beyond requirements and sound reasoning.

Within the last fifty-plus years, we as individuals and organizations have become increasingly more legalistic, and our society has become litigation stricken, if not paralyzed. I refer to this as *policy paralysis*. This paralysis hasn't affected all organizations to same extent. I do not have research to support my claim, nevertheless (1) I contend inspiring, loving, servant leadership organizations tend to not have a need for as many policies as their less-inspired and less-loving counterparts, (2) I do not believe they need to write a new policy every time a *leadership* deficiency occurs; therefore, they do not have as many policies per employee capita, and (3) they tend to create, maintain, and manage policies through more thoughtful and conservative processes.

More simply stated, inspiring, loving, servant leadership organizations create and maintain policies designed to serve two fundamental purposes: (1) they strive to provide *useful tools* for their employees, and (2) they strive to provide *protection* for their employees, rather than serving as *punitive measures*. When employees are more trusting of one another, organizations find it unnecessary to build protective walls with another policy.

Such organizations tend to focus on processes and systems, rather than trying to lay blame at the feet of their employees.

We are more apt to hear something to the effect, "Let's create a team to conduct a root cause analysis of what went wrong," rather than the knee-jerk reaction, "We better write a policy so that doesn't happen again."

We need to guard against this self-perpetuating, self-defeating cycle:

More legalistic/litigious environment→identify problems→write punitive policies to protect from litigation→policy violations occur→leads to litigation→more policies for protection from litigation→more legalistic/litigious environment. . ..

On the farm, we may have described this cycle as a *dog chasing its tail,* or asking *what came first, the chicken or the egg?*

25) Do Not Sweat the Little Things

I do not consider myself a naturally detailed-oriented individual. I have learned how to adapt, as there are times when paying attention to the details is most important. When necessary, I can transition to the detailed mode easily, without being reckless.

In my pursuit of being an inspiring, loving, servant leader, I have found it important to *not sweat the little things.* I recommend the same approach to you as the CEO, the leadership team, and other managers within your organization. Generally, it calls for sensing and finding the happy medium in given circumstances.

I will expand on one example related to dress codes. I believe it is generally important to have standardized dress code policies for organizations—within reason, of course. There may be a variety of reasons, related to encouraging team spirit and identity, safety, health, department recognition, customer identification, the nature of the job, and overall appropriateness. I will provide a short story, which will appear extreme but may be helpful in making the point. *Disclaimer:* Any resemblance of the events in this story to real life is purely intentional.

Once upon a time, there was a CEO of a medium-sized corporation. He/she was well-respected by his/her peers and was active in related professional organizations. The organization had gone to extreme measures over a period of several months to standardize company-wide dress code policies. Inspired by the CEO, there had been a high degree of staff involvement in developing and finalizing these policies. This process had been well-received throughout the organization. Staff members were taking great pride in their new uniforms. This was true of individuals, departments, and the entire company.

Shortly after the dress code initiative had been finalized and implemented, the company began to suffer financial strains. There were several examples of what may be referred to as poorly-conceived, knee-jerk cost-reducing measures being implemented. A sampling of the *all-staff email admonishments* included: run less water when washing your hands, reduce the number of paper copies being made, do not use as many paper towels, limit the number of toilet flushes, turn lights off when leaving a room (even if actively occupied)—to name only a few.

In the midst of these distractions, the CEO took it upon himself/herself to move throughout the facility with a measuring tape to determine the distance from the floor to the seam of certain uniforms, along with other variations. The purpose of this effort was to identify outliers whose uniforms were beyond the agreed-upon specifications. This prompted oral warnings, which transcended to written reprimands, which resulted in hurt feelings, loss of respect, and major distractions.

The organization had just come off of a highly inspirational undertaking—the finalization and implementation of the dress codes, inspired through the efforts of the CEO. Staff members were pleased with the final products. This was a company-wide endeavor that affected all employees throughout the entire organization. All departments had equal representation in determining not only their individual departmental uniform but also in establishing standardized dress codes for the entire organization. The employees at every level had been made to feel their opinions did count and they could influence positive outcomes in operations.

In the face of financial challenges, the leadership team lost its inspirational edge and caved to focusing on petty, insignificant cost-cutting measures. To add insult to injury, the CEO took upon himself/herself to challenge the integrity of the staff by literally lowering himself/herself to measuring uniform infractions and other minor variations of the dress code. Sadly, the focus of the staff now shifted from an inspirational high to what appeared to them as degrading, disrespectful measures.

There are several ironies to be found in this vignette:

1) As a good thing, the CEO and leadership team had inspired an entire staff by encouraging the development of uniforms and dress code policies.

2) The staff had taken pride in their accomplishments and in the final outcomes. Through a need to demonstrate control, most likely due to impending financial challenges, the CEO stooped lowly (literally and figuratively), resulting in (a) a tarnished gloss on the dress code accomplishments, (b) perpetual fodder for comments, such as *"Doesn't the CEO have more important things to do?"* and (c) a loss of respect for and confidence in the CEO and the leadership team—ironically, at a time when that confidence was most needed.

3) Often when challenges arise, such as financial ones, we as leaders immediately gravitate toward implementing less significant measures we believe we can control. Education-related expenses are often on this list of knee-jerk cost reduction measures.

This emphasis on educational-related expenses only compounds an already emotionally charged approach to reducing costs. Without appropriate explanation and delivery, employees view this as taking away a tool that they need to do their jobs. This is a difficult message when we, as leaders, have touted our commitment to being a learning organization.

4) Most employees agree it is important to conserve our natural resources, i.e., being mindful of the cost-reducing efforts above, as part of ongoing operations. Unfortunately, these normal awareness items can become tainted as petty, degrading, heavy-handed measures in the eyes of staff as a result of poor timing and ill-prepared presentation.

5) The greatest irony of all is this: We will never know for certain, but imagine a much different outcome or end to this story. If only:

a) The CEO and leadership team had practiced, promoted, and modeled inspiring, loving, servant leadership consistently through humble, mature, and ever-learning approaches, and thus,

b) The CEO and leadership team had been *more deliberate* in planning their response to the impending financial challenges, and

c) The CEO and leadership team had been *more transparent* in sharing information with other managers and the entire organization, and

d) The CEO and leadership team *had harnessed* the same momentum and buy-in they'd experienced when they inspired the organization to remodel the entire dress code policy, and

e) The CEO and leadership team *would have sought input* from all managers and front-line staff for suggestions in promoting growth and reducing reasonable and logical expenses and, finally

f) The CEO and leadership team *would have heeded* the wisdom found in, *"Learning not to sweat the little things."*

Motivation (fear-based) Scatters. Inspiration (love-based) Gathers.

26) Rid the Organization of Performance Evaluations/Rankings

One of the most demeaning, disrespectful, and useless creations we have subjected employees to in recent times is what we have affectionately referred to as Employee Evaluations, Employee Performance Reviews, or some other variation of these two. Before anyone becomes disagreeable about this, allow me to say, "I have a recommended approach which accomplishes much more through a more respectful manner, in my opinion." We will discuss this in a subsequent segment.

I will cast my observations before casting my line. At times, it is good to not only assess where we are, but also to reflect on how we got to where we are. This is one of those times.

I've said this before, *within the last fifty-plus years, we as individuals and organizations have become increasingly more legalistic and litigation-stricken, if not paralyzed.* This observation is also applicable to this discussion. This is my 10,000-foot assessment of how we have progressed to where we are today. I believe this scenario has played out with some resemblance to the following sequence:

1) One formative reason for this as it applies to this discussion is that we, as wannabe inspiring, loving, servant leaders, are the inheritors of uninspiring leaders who did not always have the best interests of their employees in mind. This does not mean they were bad people; rather, it speaks to the historical philosophies and to the differences in our places of work.

    A variety of fallout conditions caused employees to seek third-party representation in order to have a voice in determining their pay, benefits, and working conditions. To be clear, it is not my purpose to share or imply any judgements regarding third-party representation. My opinions on this subject are neutral with respect to sharing what I believe were progressive developments in our workforce environments.

2) As organizations found themselves having to deal with third-party representatives, they began seeking out and retaining legal representation, likely from outside firms initially, and eventually, more and more companies hired their own inhouse legal support. Such adaptations were also likely dependent on the size and nature of the company's business.

3) Somewhere within the fray of these developments, new processes likely began to emerge, adding sophistication to employment agreements and third-party negotiations. I am speculating that one of these early creations was the *job description.*

Job descriptions defined the requirements of the various jobs covered under third-party representation and employment agreements. Since third-party representation placed value on the output of the human component, it became more and more important for employers to be assured they were getting their money's worth, so to speak. I speculate this led to what we now affectionately recognize as *job evaluations, performance reviews,* or some variation thereof. The job description was designed to define the work being purchased, and the job evaluation was designed to measure the individual's production and the value they'd brought to the job.

4) As years passed, and the number of different jobs within an expanding number of business sectors grew exponentially, a smaller percentage of the workforce was being represented by third-party representatives and associated

agreements. By this time, employers retaining legal counsel had become a highly accepted practice, and one most organizations believed they absolutely needed to protect their interests with respect to human resources.

Speaking of human resources, I speculate it was about this same time when personnel departments (precursors to modern-day human resource departments) were being formulated within many organizations. By this time, the job description and performance evaluation forms had become fundamental to processes related to human resources; therefore, these two forms tagged along as personnel departments came into their own. Emphasis on the legal aspects of the employment relationship also carried over with many of the processes personnel departments had inherited.

5) As years continued to pass, a higher percentage of employees in the workforce were not being represented by third-party representation. We also continued to produce uninspiring leaders at a rapid rate who were weak enough to bend to the expectations of the organizations, but not strong enough to meet the inherent needs of their organization's employees. Employees continued to believe they needed something or someone to represent them to ensure their rights were being protected and their inherent needs were being met. Many employees believed their only recourse was to be found in the legal system. This is what I refer to as the *silent stand-off,* or *opposing tensions,* and it began to emerge between employees and leadership, within many organizations.

6) Organizations developed and ramped-up their own protective mechanisms in dealing with employees characterized as non-conformers, under-producers, or those with poor attitudes and/or inappropriate work behaviors; or in some cases, all of the above. This call for action resulted in more and more detailed job descriptions and corresponding job

evaluations or performance evaluations. Personnel departments became *human resource* departments, in order to connote more inclusive concern for all employee aspects.

We decided the performance evaluation form needed to correspond item-for-item with the job description, often resulting in pages on pages of each form. Leaders and human resource representatives continued to work hard at developing and promoting processes which would *be objective* in determining *subjective* work performance. To overcome this dilemma, we decided to add ranking mechanisms to each of the performance criteria. A range of 1–5 became quite popular in most circles; generally something along the lines of a "1" being "not meeting expectations" and a "5" being "exceeding expectations." Often, the total number of points would be slotted into various ranges, which would determine eligible pay adjustments.

7) Even though employees are asked to treat performance evaluation scores and corresponding pay adjustments as *confidential* and not to be shared with others, leaders need to assume just the opposite. These processes often result in pitting employee against employee; leaders struggling to explain why Jane received an overall "5" (a 4 percent adjustment) and Jan received a 4.0 (a 3 percent adjustment) or worse, a 4.5; hard feelings toward and disrespect for the leader, a lashing out of blame, reduction in self-worth, poor work attitudes, low employee morale—and a reduction in productivity were the inevitable result.

Another downfall, characteristic of many organizations, is that normally these dreaded (by both the leader and the employee) performance evaluations are conducted once per year. This is why we refer to these as annual evaluations. Often, it is during this review session when employees hear about their poor performance for the first time. This is difficult news, particularly when you have been floating along, believing you are doing a pretty good job. Through the eyes of the employee, this ranks right up there as cruel and unusual punishment. Typically, two individuals walk out of the room feeling regretful about this annual experience—the employee and the leader.

These scenarios become difficult to defend when we emphasize employees working as teams—particularly, when team members are being pitted against one another through these so-called objective ranking systems.

Another travesty may be lurking when it becomes necessary to place someone on progressive discipline, when they've received glowing performance reviews during their previous evaluations. These situations, if they end up being settled through arbitration or the legal system, are hard to defend. In my experiences, leaders attempting to be as fair and objective as possible often deliver these glowing, over-stated reviews.

8) Admittedly, I have devoted considerable time and space to providing what I believe is a reasonable synopsis of how we have progressed to where we are regarding performance reviews, a.k.a. performance appraisals. I have a great deal of respect for human resource departments and administrators. I have observed that processes associated with job descriptions and performance appraisal procedures are held closely to the hearts of those in modern-day human resource departments. I believe, however, that many will come to recognize the benefits associated with my recommendations.

In the meantime, I recommend all CEOs and leadership teams seriously consider discarding all performance review systems, particularly those which incorporate ranking measures. In my years of experience, I have never seen anything good result from these types of systems. For the inspiring, loving, servant leader, adherence to such systems is discouraging, destructive, and disrespectful; because these processes are not aligned with everything they believe and practice as such inspiring, loving, servant leaders and coaches.

It is really quite simple. All we need to do as inspiring, loving, servant leaders is to treat all others, in this case employees, consistently through an atmosphere of fairness, integrity, respect, and love. Our systems and processes will follow, becoming congruent with and reaffirming of our messages relative to inspired, loving, servant leadership. *Just do the right thing—and remind others: it is never too late to do the right thing.*

Motivation (fear-based) Scatters. Inspiration (love-based) Gathers.

27) Do Not Subject the Organization to Employee Satisfaction Surveys and Engagement Surveys

More modern-day creations are the *employee satisfaction survey* and the *employee engagement survey.* In fairness, you should know my feelings towards these surveys parallel those I have regarding employee performance evaluations/assigned rankings. My disdain for both is of equal measure.

To maintain balanced perspective, I will share the following definitions relating to both employee satisfaction and employee engagement surveys:

Employee Satisfaction:

Employee satisfaction is the extent to which employees are happy or content with their jobs and work environments.

Employee Engagement:

Employee engagement is the extent to which employees feel compassionate about their jobs, are committed to the organization, and invest discretionary effort into their work.

Would it surprise you if I told you, given a culture which subscribes to and practices inspiring, loving, servant leadership in its purest of forms, it is absolutely unnecessary (and often inappropriate) to employ an outside agency to conduct an employee satisfaction or an employee engagement survey throughout your organization?

Even if your organization is a *runner-up,* meaning you are *running-up and towards* being such an organization, I would say the same thing. Having made the commitment as a CEO and leadership team to become inspired, loving, servant leaders—and thus, an inspiring, loving, servant leadership organization—places your organization one or two laps ahead of those who have not made that commitment. Let us be reminded, everyone in the organization is a leader.

Please consider these observations and conclusions:

a) In my opinion, employee satisfaction surveys and employee engagement surveys are to departments and specific work units, what employee performance ranking evaluations are to individual employees. These surveys can also create divisiveness, internal competition for resources, hard feelings, and ironically, lower morale and confidence in leadership and in the organization—and a reduction in productivity follows.

    We expect employees to work in teams. Similarly, we expect departments to work as one large team on behalf of the organization. These persuasions and the potential fallout of employee satisfaction and engagement surveys are often inconsistent and potentially detrimental to the organization.

b) There is little (and mixed) data and information to suggest either of these presumed tools directly results in or contributes to improved organizational performance.

c) As the CEO and leadership team, why should you pay a significant fee to an outside agency to inhabit your organization for a short period of time and do what you and you team should be doing day in and day out, on an ongoing basis? Ultimately, the CEO and the leadership team are accountable for addressing all actual and perceived problems and inadequacies exposed by this outside agency. *Perception* and *reality* need to be treated the same. You may even need to *mend some fences* before you consider grazing the flock. By this, I suggest you will need to address hard feelings, lack of trust, and other fallout conditions of the survey, before you can begin addressing the output of the survey itself.

I cannot resist the opportunity to share two analogies:

The first analogy: I view the agency as coming into the organization, placing two fingers on the radial artery of the organization, and subsequently reporting the pulse rate as one rate at a given time. On the other hand, I liken the CEO and leadership team to continuous-read heart rate monitors. Each of you as inspired, loving, servant leaders are capable of reporting the organization's pulse rate at any given time, over a period of time. This is your job. *Walk your halls and be with your people; and if you are caring and perceptive at all, you will know if they are satisfied and engaged—or not.*

The second analogy: (just in case you did not relate to the first) I liken the agency to a still-image camera, which captures one image at a given time. On the other hand, the CEO and the leadership team, as inspired, loving, servant leaders, function like video cameras, since they capture a multitude of images at various times, over a period time—on an ongoing basis. A video reveals much more information about the subject than a single-frame picture. This is your job. *Walk your halls and be with your people; and if you are caring and perceptive at all, you will know if they are satisfied and engaged—or not.*

d) Lance Secretan, in his latest book, *The Bellwether Effect*, reminds us *the employee is the new customer.* Now, as you walk your halls, the view through this lens of *employee as customer,* takes on a new and refreshing perspective, does it not?

e) To their credit, agencies who sponsor the employee satisfaction and employee engagement surveys generally work hard in trying to assure anonymity within the gathering of information and the reporting-out processes. In smaller organizations, preserving such anonymity is a challenge, due to the smaller size of many departments. As such, since some employees do not fully trust being able to remain anonymous, they often skew their demographic information, which, in turn, may mischaracterize certain outcomes.

f) Admittedly, a symptom of uninspiring cultures is poor or lack of communication, from both the employee to the leader, and from the leader to the employee. In more desirable settings, this would ideally be described as highly interactive, respectful, and loving conversation between the two parties, the employee and the leader. Even though there may be good reasons why the ability to communicate effectively has eroded between the employee and leader, this does not relieve either party from his/her responsibility to do their part in communicating effectively with one another.

   One aspect of the employee surveys I do not approve of is the opportunity it provides to the unhappy, disgruntled employee to make anonymous, disrespectful, one-sided comments about his/her leader, which are often disparaging of the leader. This opportunity is taken *as the path of least resistance,* or what we loosely describe as a "cheap shot" or "an end run."

g) I will not speculate on average costs associated with implementing and managing an employee satisfaction survey and/or an employee engagement survey. These costs typically vary with the size of the organization and the extent of services proffered. In addition to the fees paid to the agency directly, there are considerable hidden costs associated with managing and completing immediate and ongoing follow-up within the organization.

Even though I cannot estimate your total costs in conducting either or both of these types of surveys, I am confident in saying there are much better ways to invest the same amount of money, in my opinion. There are a number of inspirational undertakings the CEO and leadership team could initiate, which would be reflective of your actions as inspiring, loving, servant leaders striving to create a culture, reflective of these characteristics. It will be up to you, as a leadership team with representative input, to determine what these options might be. I will offer the following criteria for your consideration, in making these decisions.

The initiatives and associated experiences should:

1) Be wholesome, pure, and reflective of the culture you are striving to create—and characterized as inspiring, caring, and loving, as expressed through the *heart of a servant.*
2) Be available and provided to *everyone* in the organization, regardless of position or rank. I also suggest board members be included.
3) Be simple and not overly complicated. Ensure your choices will not be so intricate as to topple under their own weight.
4) Be introduced and conducted in such a way everyone can share the same experiences simultaneously; if not at the same time, within a short period of time. Shared experiences tend to produce shared buy-in, commitment, conviction, and accountability.

5) Be conducted via a platform of organizational cross-representation, rather than by departments or work units.

6) Be provided as a paid-time activity. This is not only a likely requirement, but it is the right thing to do. It reinforces the message that the leadership team, and entire organization, considers this effort to be important and a priority.

7) Finally, starting with the commitment of the leadership team to subscribe to and model inspiring, loving, servant leadership, it is important all of the criteria outlined above be approved and supported by the leadership team, by consensus.

I will take this opportunity to share a personal experience, which answered the specifications of each of the above criteria:

On the heels of our leadership team having committed to becoming more inspiring, loving, servant leaders, we made arrangements with Lance Secretan, internationally known author and speaker (as introduced previously), to be on our campus for one long, full day.

We promoted Lance's visit with typical pre-billing information distributed through the management staff face-to-face and by email. We invited *everyone* in the entire organization, including the medical staff and the board of directors.

Ideally, it would have been best to have had everyone attend the same presentation as a shared experience. This was not possible, due to the nature of the hospital's work. The next best thing was to provide two, four-hour presentations, one in the morning and the other in the afternoon of the same day. We made it clear everyone would be paid for the entire four hours.

Though we did not want to use the term, *required attendance,* it was implied we expected everyone to make this a high priority, reinforced with this being paid-time. With the exception of four or five employees who were on vacation or sick leave at the time, all other employees attended one of the two sessions.

In addition to this event as a wonderful personal and organizational experience, we also wanted to honor and pamper the attendees with typical conference amenities, including a continental breakfast for the morning group and freshly-baked cookies for the afternoon group, all accompanied with a selection of beverages.

For some of the staff, this was the first time they had attended such an inspiring, educational event, so we wanted to make it very nice in content and presentation. We also provided an overlapping buffet luncheon for both the morning and afternoon groups. Sharing food together, in and of itself, complemented the spirit of the day. Given the hospital's twenty-four hour, seven days/week operation, many of the staff had not met each other, beyond telephone interactions. For many, this was an opportunity to establish new relationships.

In preparation, we rented a high-definition audio and video system, complemented with a large-screen system to ensure presentation quality. Our emphasis was not only on high-grade equipment but also on hiring professional technical support for proper set-up and effective operations.

The big day was fast approaching. Lance arrived the afternoon before the presentations. The leadership team, in addition to the president of the board, met with Lance over dinner the preceding evening. Not only was this a good opportunity to become better acquainted, it also provided an opportunity for Lance to witness and assess the strength of our convictions, as a team, in becoming more inspiring, loving, servant leaders—and in promoting an organizational culture characteristic of the same.

During dinner, I remember asking Lance what was the largest group he had ever addressed. In his humble manner, he replied, 35,000! I was (we were) not only humbled, but especially honored, that he would be providing the same messages to our small organization as he presents to the masses.

The next day proved to be a day I will always remember, appreciate, and for which I remain eternally grateful as a highlight of my career. This was a wonderful day, yielding outcomes beyond our expectations. As leaders, how often are we afforded a real-life experience where *all* employees, representing cross-sections of socio-economic and educational backgrounds and positions throughout the organization, along with physicians, board members, leadership, and management come together as human beings, all on the same level? Titles were all checked at the door, so to speak. It was heartwarming to witness front-line employees, board members, physicians, managers, and members of the leadership team interspersed throughout the audiences, sitting next to one another during the presentations and chatting over lunch.

This was all made possible through Lance's interactive approach with both audiences, cementing his most inspiring message. I believe he *lit a fire* within each person that day, in tribute to his definition of inspiration. In referencing the *Pebble Theory* from an earlier discussion, we will never know the full extent this day impacted others—at work, at home, and at play.

As I boil everything else away about this day, I will remember the riveting image of Lance modeling what it is looks like to be an inspiring, loving, servant leader.

I offer this experience as one example of an initiative I believe exceeded the previous criteria I'd set forth. There are other experiences you may choose for your organization. Given an equal amount of money to be invested in either (1) our experiences with Lance Secretan versus (2) retaining an outside agency to conduct an employee satisfaction survey and/or employee engagement survey, hands down and without a second thought, I would choose the experience with Lance. The fires set by either of these surveys will ignite; consume; and be quickly smothered, leaving messy ashes behind; while the fires ignited (the spark) within each of us by Lance, will continue to burn (the flame) and provide light for others.

Motivation (fear-based) Scatters. Inspiration (love-based) Gathers.

28) Dreams/Values; Not Mission, Vision, and Values

As inspiring, loving, servant leaders, I recommend we become more comfortable in speaking of *dreams*, instead of mission and vision, the magical dyad most organizations believe their employees should embrace. Even though most cannot recite it, if asked spontaneously without time to reference or prepare. Making this change should become a movement.

Continued emphasis on these two organizational components is an example of being steeped in the rigidity of tradition. Most find it easier and more acceptable to perpetuate what we have always done, *or* modify it slightly, than it is to stretch and create something new—a whole new platform and way of thinking about something. Hours upon hours (and dollars on dollars) are consumed by many organizations in defining this dyad, only to be shelved and forgotten in time. The most disappointing condition is these two individually, and both collectively, contribute little, if anything, to improving the culture and/or performance of the organization.

During my career, I have experienced several group opportunities to struggle with drafting this dyad of mission and vision statements. Admittedly and predictably, prior to drafting and agreeing on these associated statements, we found ourselves needing to first review the definition and distinction of each, along with their connectivity. I have found these processes have a tendency to suffer collapse under their own weight, again with little positive effect on overall performance.

In an effort to remain objective in my convictions regarding the dyad, I've conducted an abbreviated search *of* and *for* meaning. I have gathered a series of definitions and associated information, which I've found helpful. Please note the cyclical nature of the highlighted sections, in which the word being defined or referenced is also repeatedly found in the definitions of the other member of the dyad, and vice versa. No wonder, many find the distinctions and interconnectivity within the dyad confusing and meaningless in promoting an inspiring culture and improved performance.

I believe the collection of information below is important. I also believe we can preserve the perceived purpose and value of the dyad through a simpler, more manageable, and meaningful manner. Please review with me:

Mission

Mission Statement (definition): a formal summary of the aims and values of a company, organization, or individual.

Source: *Marketing Blender:* "A mission statement is a formal summary of values of an organization. We describe it as the *Doing* piece—it describes how you act as a servant leader. It proclaims who you serve, what you serve, and how you do it every day."

Vision

Vision Statement (definition): a statement of what a company or an organization would like to achieve in the future.

Source: *Marketing Blender:* "A vision statement is a declaration of an organization's overarching objective or goal. We refer to it as the *Dreaming* piece—if everything goes right, it is how your organization will change the world."
Source: *Vision Statement Definition with Vision Statement Examples,* By: Susan Ward, May 20, 2019:

> A vision statement is sometimes called a picture of your company in the future, but it's so much more than that.

Your vision statement is your inspiration, the framework for all your strategic planning.

What you are doing when creating a vision statement is articulating your dreams and hopes for your business. Your vision statement describes what you are trying to build and serves as a touchstone for your future actions. As the *Marketing Blender* puts it, *"Your vision statement should be an audacious dream of a future reality* based on the work you do . . .. *Your vision should require people to dream."* (emphasis added)

The vision statement is not tied to the details. That's why *it's important that a vision statement captures your passion.* The vision statement is not about soaring; the poring over ways and means to accomplish the vision comes after.
— Susan Ward

Dream Statement (definition): A cherished aspiration, ambition, or ideal.

Source: *CommunityToolBox: Proclaiming Your Dream: Developing Vision and Mission Statements.*

Your vision is your dream. Whatever your organization's dream is, it may be well articulated by one or more vision statements, which are short phrases or sentences that convey your community's hope for the future.
Ref: CommunityToolBox

Values

Value Statement (definition): a statement of the *desirability of something:* (1) *the regard that something is held to deserve;* the importance, worth, or usefulness of something; (2) a person's *principles or standards of behavior;* one's judgment of *what is important* in life.

Value Statement: An organization's statement of its ethical values that is complementary to mission statement and vision statement.

Based on my findings above, I am recommending—rather than equating, qualifying, and connecting—I am suggesting we combine these statements into one term, *Dream/Values,* as follows:

Mission statement + **Vision** statement + **Values** statement = **Dream/Values** statement

This new *Dream* terminology will be more meaningful and inspirational for employees to understand, support, embellish, and identify with through their roles—resulting in more inspired, higher performing organizations. In support of my conclusion, I ask who personally has not made one of these statements, or said something similar, "I have always had a dream to . . ." or "I have always dreamed of this happening"? We know what it is to have a dream. This country has been built on the realization and fulfillment of dreams at all levels, from personal to corporate and beyond.

29) Develop a "Rear-View Mirror" and "Windshield" Model

I promised to discuss what I believe is an ideal approach in replacing the traditional Performance Ranking Appraisals many organizations continue to propagate. I believe these recommendations naturally flow from, and integrate well, with my arguments for promoting organizational dreams—instead of mission and vision—as discussed in the previous section.

I am speaking primarily to CEOs and leadership teams in sharing my premises regarding these transitions from *Mission, Vision,* and *Values* to *Dreams/Values* and from *Performance*

Ranking Appraisals to *Personal Dreams,* all of which integrate well in a hand and glove relationship. This will require an open-minded, transparent, and candid discussion by the leadership team. Consensus and total, undivided support and promotion will be necessary as a true litmus test for the team functioning as a team. Predictably, there will be some who are hesitant to move away from the false comfort provided by the traditional dyad on an organizational level, and performance ranking appraisals on an individual employee level. This may prove to be a particularly difficult transition for human resource executives.

I urge leadership teams to be progressive in making this bold, but monumental, decision. The leadership team needs to coach the other managers along in this process to assure the same buy-in, support, and promotion. Staff, at all levels, will thank you for it, and you will feel much better about your role as inspiring, loving, servant leaders.

It may be helpful, but not required, to have your *Dream/ Values* statement in place prior to launching this initiative. I will be suggesting a phase-in plan which will make this change more comfortable for the organization. For the purposes of this discussion, let's assume you have finalized your Dream/ Values statement.

These are some of the major tenets of the *Rear-View Mirror* and *Windshield* model and their associated review process:

1) Rather than meeting annually for the performance ranking appraisal, emphasize meeting at least quarterly with the employee to see if they need assistance in meeting their personal dreams and contributions to the organizational dream. This is an opportunity to identify barriers and provide feedback to the employee regarding the status of their dreams. The tenor of these *discussions* is much different than that of the annual appraisals.

2) In rolling this out to staff, it should be presented as a process in which there is a transition of influence from the manager to the employee. The employees will assume more responsibility in sharing the management and accomplishment of their dreams, with the support and encouragement of their managers. This is also a good time to discuss the organizational Dream/Values statement.

3) Your organization can design a format which is best suited for your organization. I recommend this entire process be managed throughout the year on a one-page form, electronically, in hard copy, or both as needed. Personally, I suggest utilizing an electronic version, as this facilitates the statement becoming a *living* document to be shared back and forth between the employee and servant leader. Doing so also allows for free-texting, as needed. If necessary, it is appropriate for this *live document* to extend to a second page or more.

   With respect to the layout and content, I prefer to devote the top-half of the page to the *Rear-View Mirror* (backward looking) portion and the second half to the *Windshield* portion (forward looking). From the beginning, I suggest an emphasis on keeping the format and the process as simple and as streamlined as possible. I am providing the following outline of the format I have found helpful in managing this process. This is only intended to serve as a sample for your consideration:

Name of the Organization
Rear-View Mirror and Windshield Record
Quarterly Discussions
Fiscal Year '22 (7/1/21 — 6/30/22)

Organizational Dream/Values Statement: _______________________________

____

Rear View Mirror: (Accomplishments I am proud of this year.)
a) Personal Dreams:

    1. ____

    2. ____

Comments: ____

b) Work-Related Dreams:

    1. ____

    2. ____

Comments: ____

Windshield: (Things I want to accomplish this next year.)
a) Personal Dreams:

    1. ____

    2. ____

Comments: ____

b) Work-Related Dreams:

    1. ____

    2. ____

Comments: ____

c) As servant leader, are there things I can do to support you in accomplishing
your dreams?____

Employee: _________________________________ Date: _____________

Servant Leader:_______________________________ Date: _____________

4) After rolling out the new system to all staff throughout the entire organization, you are now prepared to take the first step in the transition process. This first step is to meet with each employee and ask them to select both personal and work-related dreams. You may need to provide some time for their consideration, since this is a new process.

When you meet to finalize their dreams for this next fiscal year, be prepared to discuss these in more detail, provide guidance, and identify things you can do to be supportive throughout the next fiscal year. Please remember to model a tenor and spirit consistent with an inspiring, loving, two-way conversation. This step would generally be completed during the last few weeks of the current fiscal year.

5) Now that each employee and their respective servant leader have together finalized the employee's dreams for the upcoming fiscal year, the next step will occur at the end of the first quarter. Discussions between the employee and the servant leader can and should occur on an informal, ongoing basis.

These recommended *check-ins,* or quarterly review sessions, must occur so there is no lost time in helping the employee accomplish their dreams. This is also a time when brief notes should be recorded and initialed, documenting these informal review sessions and notable progress.

These mentoring sessions should be scheduled towards the end of quarters 1, 2, 3, and 4. During the fourth quarterly review, the dreams (and notations) should be electronically moved from the *Windshield* section to the *Rear-View Mirror* section. This last session of the year will provide two opportunities for the employee and servant leader to: (1) review the year-end dream accomplishments, and (2) begin the process of identifying dreams for the next fiscal year; closing-out one chapter and opening the next.

I trust each of you, as employee and servant leader, will find these conversations more comfortable and relaxing than the traditional performance ranking appraisal sessions, which were fear-based. My hope is both parties will leave the conversation feeling more inspired to make positive changes in the lives of those we have been called to serve—and one another.

Motivation (fear-based) Scatters. Inspiration (love-based) Gathers.

30) Treat Well . . . Hire Well . . . and Then Treat Well

I have placed emphasis on creating an inspiring, loving, servant leader organization. I have also spoken directly to CEOs and leadership teams concerning their roles in establishing such a culture. We have discussed the need to first, inspire ourselves *(The Spark)* so we in turn can coach and inspire others *(The Flame)*. I have spoken often about all of us being leaders, facilitators, and ambassadors within our organizations. All of us should hold ourselves accountable in doing our part to be inspiring, loving, servant leaders.

Since we have discussed personal dreams, work-related dreams, and overall organizational *Dream/Values* statements, we will discuss several suggestions relating to hiring principles and practices. These initiatives are to be implemented in an effort to establish an inspiring, loving, servant leader organization. We not only owe this to our existing employees; we should feel obligated to provide the same to new hires as well. As a reminder, I have included individuals seeking employment in high performing, inspirational cultures on my intended audience list.

This cause and effect illustration emulates the following chain of events, in such cultures being envisioned:

Inspiring, Loving, Servant Leaders *develop and promote* Inspiring, Loving, Servant Leader Organizations *which become strong corporate citizens and attract* Good Talent *through sound recruitment practices, and hire* Qualified, Inspiring, and Loving Employees *who create dream-filled* Inspiring, Loving Cultures *which develop* Inspiring, Loving, Servant Leaders *who inspire, love, serve, coach, develop, retain, and celebrate* Inspiring, Loving, Servant Employees *through sound retention practices who become* Informal Leaders, Facilitators, and Ambassadors *dedicated to and remaining with the organization to promote* Dreaming, Inspiring, Loving Cultures *which become* High-Performing/High-Producing/Growing Organizations *comprised of creative and* inspiring, Loving Servants *who create, promote, and fulfill personal and organizational dreams and attract* Good Talent . . . *and so on, as the cycle repeats itself.*

This may unfold and sound like a fairy tale, but I assure you this can be a real-life, cause and effect scenario in your organization.

My purpose is to share the *whats* and *whys* and not the *hows*. I trust inspiring, loving, servant leaders are fully capable of designing and tailoring practices best suited to their respective organizations.

I want to provide a few thoughts and considerations important to hiring and retaining good talent:

1) Be committed and strongly convicted to (a) becoming an inspiring, loving CEO and leadership team, and (b) building a culture and organization worthy and characteristic of those convictions. Remember, this is not a new fad management model, it is a way of doing *your* business, built on sound and timeless principles and practices.

2) In addition to being committed and convicted, you and your team will need to be patient and deliberate.

Building these cultures require a generous supply of both. Remember, *the value of the juice far exceeds the effort of the squeeze*—and potentially, that value will endure the passage of time long after you leave the organization.

3) Another important commitment your leadership team needs to adhere to is *always hiring right and hiring well.* We made it a practice many years ago to *never just settle, regardless of the amount of time required to fill the position with a qualified candidate.*

Hiring an employee is the creation of a contractual relationship between two parties that is intended to represent the interests of both parties. Interviewing and hiring processes are designed to select and place the most qualified candidate in the selected position and associated role. On behalf of the organizations we represent, we tend to look at hiring primarily from the perspective of finding what is best for our organization, without regard for what is best for the new hire. As servant leaders, we need to feel obligated to do the right thing on behalf of the new hire as well. The old adage applies here, *If it isn't good for both parties, it probably is not good for either party.*

We all know collective processes associated with recruiting, interviewing, hiring, background checking, orienting, and training are costly for the organization. High turnover rates add a multiplier effect to these costs. Maintaining turnover at a lower rate in inspiring, loving, servant leader organizations translates to a significant reduction in hiring-related costs.

Seeking, accepting, and starting a new job may be an expensive endeavor for the candidate as well. This may be reflected in direct financial costs and more indirect sacrifices associated with moving expenses, temporary housing, uprooting family, moving long distances, or leaving family behind. Inspiring, loving, servant leaders consider the significance of these conditions out of respect for the individual candidate. *We must work towards getting it right every time.*

4) Ideally, we should hire the most qualified individuals based on skills, behaviors, and attitudes. I have simplified these qualities as skills and *behavitudes*. If I had to choose between these two qualities, I would consistently choose *behavitudes* over skills. Organizations can generally train for skills, but it is difficult to change behavior and attitudes. *We must work towards getting it right every time.*

5) With respect to the selection process, I suggest involving peer staff in the entire process. This will involve reviewing applications, participating in the interview process, and being asked to provide feedback to human resources and the respective hiring leader. Depending on the nature of the position, there are many approaches to this overall endeavor. You will choose processes best suited for your organization.

Your focus should be on good organization, hospitality, structure, consistency, and comfortable/inviting settings, in addition to eliciting appropriate representation and feedback. This is a great opportunity to model hospitality to everyone in the room, not just the applicant. Not only will staff be inspired with their sense of ownership, it will also be a good opportunity for you and other leaders to impart organizational information and model inspiring, loving, servant leadership—not only for the applicant, but for all participating employees, as witnesses to your testimonies. *Repetition leads to reinforcement; reinforcement leads to remembrance; remembrance leads to repetition, and so on . . .* until one day, you hear employees sharing the same things you have often professed as truisms.

All of the things listed above are important when it comes to treating applicants with respect and dignity.

Early in my career, I interviewed with a small hospital system for the CEO position. Everything had gone well from my perspective, up to the day of my in-person interview. I was told I was one of three finalists for the position.

I had visited with a number of individuals during the early part of the morning. The big, group interview was scheduled for 11:00 A.M. I was not surprised with the size of the group, which numbered approximately fifteen individuals. This interview group was comprised of the chairman and other board members, members of the leadership team, department directors, physicians, and a couple of staff members.

All of these individuals were seated around a long, rectangular table. I quickly realized I had been relegated to the head of the table—my own little table at the end of the much higher, larger table. My little table had a surface top measuring approximately 2.0 ft. x 2.0 ft., just large enough for my open, black leather-bound notebook to rest. As implied, the top of my little table was approximately six inches below that of the larger table. It was positioned against the end of the large table. I immediately had flash-backs of the first Thanksgiving past when I had finally graduated from the children's table to the much larger, adult table and how good it made me feel. Now, I was seated back at the children's table.

The best was yet to come. I am a little over 6 feet 1 inch tall—not a person of small size or short stature. I could barely get my legs under the table, even though they were pressed tightly together up and under this little, wobbly table. I also remember steadying the table with my legs.

To this day, I wonder if this was an attempt to see how I would respond under pressure, intimidation—or just a byproduct of poor planning. I found it ironic, as the space occupied by my little table was greater than the space that would have been required by my chair with me seated in it . . . at the head of the table. I recall little about the interview or the rest of the day, but I will always remember how I was made to feel—very disrespected. When the offer arrived, I was pleased to decline it—though I declined with a mustered spirit of respect and appreciation for the consideration and offer.

All of the above listed details regarding a good interview *are* important, with attention to detail and dignity—regardless of the status of the position. *We must work towards getting it right every time.*

6) We, as individuals and organizations, have one opportunity to make a good first, and often lasting, impression. We should remember this, not only with our most qualified candidates, but for all applicants for each of our positions. As inspiring, loving, servant leaders, we must insist on being as respectful and responsive with those not being considered or selected for our positions. We are all ambassadors on behalf of our organization. Most individuals who have not received a job offer will *remain respectful* of the organization, providing they have been treated *respectfully*.

Job applicants are also our customers. Most job applicants in our market and service areas are also traditional customers who will select one of three options: They will speak negatively, remain neutral, or speak positively about their experiences with our organization. If their experience has been positive, they may apply at a later time for another position they are better qualified for.

Several years ago, I attended a conference focused on promotion and marketing of services. One of the speakers asserted he believed each of us has a sphere of approximately 250 people who we can influence in a negative or positive manner. He commented he had arrived at this conclusion in a very scientific manner. He relayed he had a friend who was a mortician. This mortician friend had shared that the average number of funeral service pamphlets most families ordered was 250. From this he, the speaker and friend of the mortician, substantiated his hypothesis. This has remained with me. The 250 is significant, but the number becomes astronomical when you imagine each of our 250 (arbitrary number of employees) individuals having another 250 individuals who they may influence negatively or positively. *We must work towards getting it right every time.*

7) Regarding the new hires, as inspiring, loving, servant leaders you will be committed to getting everyone off to a good start, beginning with their first day of orientation. It is an excellent time for the CEO and the rest of the leadership team to be the first to greet and officially welcome the new hires. You will develop these settings and procedures in a manner best suited for your organization. For example, the leadership team may host a luncheon for all new hires and orientation presenters on their first day. It is an excellent time for the team and all others to model what an inspiring, loving, servant leadership culture looks like. *We must work towards getting it right every time.*

8) Invest in new hires through structured orientation and training programs. Doing so conveys a strong message to new hires that you and the organization are committed to preparing them for the positions they have been hired to master. I believe it is good to complete the orientation segment prior to the new employees' assignment to their work areas. Once they become involved in their day-to-day duties and responsibilities, it may be difficult to have them leave the work area. Training programs, on the other hand, can generally be integrated with duties and responsibilities in their respective work area.

As discussed previously, an inspiring, loving, servant leader culture, subscribes to the principles of and positions itself as a learning organization. Speaking on behalf of the new hires, and all staff members, this commitment is to be modeled throughout the entire organization on an ongoing basis. It is important to involve new-hires in these ongoing educational opportunities. *We must work towards getting it right every time.*

9) Always compensate (via wages and benefits) your most important resource—the staff—fairly, equally, equitably, competitively, and without prejudice. To the extent possible, structure your compensation program around available, timely market information and cost of living information.

Several years ago, as the new CEO, I'd inherited an organization which had not experienced any type of salary adjustment for three years. Such a resulting disparity can be difficult to overcome and generally requires several baby step adjustments over a period of time. There is a cost associated with everything, either directly or indirectly. Regarding these circumstances, the money saved in salaries was offset with costs associated with higher turnover, temporary staff, contract staff, reduced morale, and lower productivity. *We must work towards getting it right every time.*

Motivation (fear-based) Scatters. Inspiration (love-based) Gathers.

31) Growth Mode More Fun Than Retraction Mode

Inspiring, loving, servant leader organizations generally experience horizontal and vertical growth proportional to their level of maturity as inspiring, loving, servant leader cultures. However, due to unique issues in their external environments, which may be beyond their control, there are no guarantees.

Even though I do not have scientific cause and effect studies to prove my point beyond a reasonable doubt, I am extremely confident in telling you I have experienced this relationship in every organization I have served. In the same breath, as humbly as possible, I am quick to always credit the many who have made this possible. I arrive at two conclusions: *First*, it is much more *fun* to *fun*ction in a growth mode, rather than a retraction mode; and *second*, against the background of always crediting others for these successes, I will only credit myself for being a champion for *growing* inspiring, loving, servant leader cultures and organizations. For me, this rewarding personal gratification is found in *three* types of growth, (1) the *personal growth* I observe on the faces and in the spirits of inspiring, loving, servant leaders and staff, (2) the *organizational growth* and *improvements*, I observe in the dreams, quality initiatives, systems, processes, measures in caring for one another, and working together in teams, and (3) the *pure vertical and horizontal growth,* as measured in volume and financial metrics, along with new programs and services. I feel blessed to have shared these experiences with many. These are experiences I hope for on your behalf, as inspiring, loving, servant leaders and staff members. These are some of the most gratifying *growth* experiences for those who love and care for others—and the organizations they serve.

Following are other aspects associated with growing organizations: *Growth is always good.*

1) *Aspire and inspire to a growth mentality.*

   Inspired, loving, servant leaders should be in the business of creating excitement (and work) throughout the organization—witnessing the excitement of others in improving quality and performance metrics, creating new programs and new services, developing and employing new technologies, adding value to existing services, growing existing and new services, and improving the financial health of the organization.

I remember sharing this with the leadership team, as we were becoming better acquainted during our early days together, *"One thing you do need to know about me, is I create a great deal of work for those around me."* This was my approach in expressing what I described in the previous paragraph. I've been pleased to be reminded of this in the months and years to come. *Growth is always good.*

2) *Develop the organizational story as it unfolds and always be prepared to share it with others.*

   As individuals, our earthly life stories begin when we inhale our first breath here on earth and continue until we exhale our last breath. For the most part, our earthly life stories are linear in nature and highly dependent on, and influenced by, a more consistent cast of characters along the way.

   Figuratively speaking, organizations also have life stories. The life story of an organization tends to be more cyclic in nature, as leaders move in and out of an organization and the cast is perpetually changing. Regardless of our position within an organization, we are all cast members for a period of time.

   In "Writing the Next Chapter," we discussed how we may want to be remembered personally and professionally. I stand by the merits of being inspiring, loving, servants and servant leaders. I suggest each of us bearing this description will have more fun, be more fulfilled, and experience personal gratification as we draft our personal and organizational stories.

   Organizations that are characterized as embracing inspiring, loving, servant leadership cultures, will reap the three types of organizational growth beyond their wildest dreams—personal and work-related. I contend *we become what we think about, talk about, dream about, and profess to be important.* This applies to both individuals and organizations.

I am reminded of my early days with Bryan Memorial Hospital. Our vertical and horizontal growth had mushroomed beyond our dreams and best-laid plans. As technologies emerged at an astonishing rate, we found it necessary to fabricate many support equipment items. As the executive director of several ancillary departments at the time, I worked closely with Mr. Harold Kelly, our director of plant operations.

In addition to being a skilled tradesman, Harold exercised an imaginative, inventive mind. One might also describe Harold as an easy-going, likeable and, most importantly, an inspiring man who treated the staff accordingly in great measure. I learned many things from Harold as we worked together on numerous projects. I will always remember Harold saying this to me, "Rog, I can build anything you can draw." Being a humble man, I believe he may have been saying, *"I can build anything you can imagine or dream of, but drawing makes it much easier for me to build."*

I say to each of you, and to all of you collectively, *"We can build cultures and organizations for tomorrow, beyond those we can only imagine and dream about today; but drawing makes it much easier for us to build."* Inspiring, loving, servant leaders need to be transparent in describing and drawing what has happened, what is happening, and what will be happening as your organizational stories unfold. As servant leaders, we need to generate excitement, creativity, support, and a sense of camaraderie and ownership throughout the entire organization. *Light it up and no one will feel they are in the dark. Growth is always good.*

3) *Be in the business of growing people and the organization will follow.*
This assertion is closely related to another I have previously shared, which applies to all types of business, industrial, and service organizations: All of us should view *our basic business as one of building collaborative relationships, with the realization that good things fall out of good relationships.* It is one thing for us to agree to cooperate; it is quite another, to agree to co-labor with one another.

Being in the business of growing people, the organization will follow. This is just one of the good things that falls out of building collaborative relationships. Inspired, loving, servant leaders *grow* employees through the creation of inspiring cultures; consequently, employees enjoy co-laboring with one another for common causes—such as improved quality, productivity, financial, and other performance metrics. *Growth is always good.*

4) *Do the right things, and the money will follow.*
Inspired, loving, servant leader cultures endear healthy organizations and healthy organizations embrace the highest of legal, ethical, and moral standards. Such organizations closely monitor financial benchmarks; however, they tend to consider positive financial metrics as the *effect*, the outcome, instead of the *cause* or driving force.

This tends to be the effect, due to the confidence they place in their inspirational cultures, servant leadership, and front-line staff for having the best interests of the organization at heart. They believe in (1) growing people (employees) and the organization will follow, and (2) do the right things, and the money will follow. For these organizations, it is not *all* about the money. *Growth is always good.*

5) *A rising tide lifts all boats.*

The aphorism, *"A rising tide lifts all boats"* is often associated with the idea that an improved economy will benefit all participants. This phrase is commonly attributed to John F. Kennedy, who used it in a 1963 speech. Ted Sorensen, Kennedy's speechwriter, would later note this was not his original phrase, or that of President Kennedy. Sorensen mused that he had borrowed it from a slogan he observed being used by the regional chamber of commerce, the New England Council. President Kennedy is credited as using this slogan often.

I am taking the liberty of also borrowing this phrase to illustrate two slightly different scenarios. The *first* scenario relates to a newly-formulated leadership team, the members of which are working hard to establish themselves as inspiring, loving, servant leaders. In previous discussions, I had recommended the team identify an initiative, which would involve all departments, and essentially all employees, within the organization.

As a personal experience, I had shared that our leadership team embarked on a hospital-wide quality performance improvement initiative. Our ultimate goal was to achieve DNV Accreditation, an internationally recognized achievement. In order to achieve this status, every department would need to play a significant role, in having their boat lifted.

The leadership team, through its commitment to change the culture, was successful in introducing, garnering support and commitment, and implementing this initiative—and in hosting a hospital-wide celebration of this accomplishment a few months later. In this vignette, this hospital-wide initiative (the tide) lifted the quality performance of all boats (every department).

The *second* scenario pertains to an organization more mature in its journey as an inspiring, loving, servant leader culture and associated organization. Through various illustrations, I have shared examples of accomplishments only made possible through the collective efforts of all departments and employees. As is typical within inspiring organizations, departments are dependent on another to be successful and do not operate on a mutually-exclusive basis. These departments work together in a collaborative fashion, and successful measures in specific departments actually lift other departments through their supportive roles. In this scenario, the success of the individual departments (the tide) lifts all supportive departments (all boats), and the entire organization is benefited. Success begets success. *Growth is always good.*

6) *You never know what will ring the bell.*
   I am compelled to share a glimpse of personal insight I believe is a product of my humble, rural upbringing. This has served me well throughout my life, though it has often made me the butt of innocent joking: *I have always enjoyed making something out of nothing.* Perhaps, a more complimentary approach would be to describe myself as always striving to be resourceful, given limited resources.

   Growing up, I was the guy who thought Velveeta cheese was the only kind of cheese. I did not learn differently until I went off to college. You can imagine my dismay when I was told Velveeta is not a cheese, but a spread.

   One of my earliest memories of *making something out nothing* was when I made farm toys out of scrap lumber, old nails, and bailing wire. This is when it all started, progressing through the years from building farm toys, to refurbishing/constructing farm implements, to revitalizing a respiratory therapy department, to flipping houses before it became the rage, to creating programs/services *on a financial shoestring* within hospitals/health systems identified as having untapped potential.

You never know what will ring the bell. Admittedly, my convictions regarding this particular slogan stem from my experiences in healthcare. I believe it also applies to all businesses, industries, and other service organizations. Disclosures: *First,* I was blessed to have been employed with organizations who focused *first,* on the healthcare needs of those within their service areas; and *second,* on the financial health of the organization. This is not to imply they were fiscally irresponsible; rather, it is to compliment them for having balanced perspectives. With guidance, they were always open to all types of vertical and horizontal growth.

Second, the significance of this slogan increased proportionally with vertical and horizontal growth. For the sake of discussion, I offer one example each of vertical growth and horizontal growth.

Vertical growth: We added orthopedic joint replacement surgery to our surgery services department.

Horizontal growth: We established six rural satellite medical clinics within a period of four years. (The driving distance from one clinic to the next to the next was over 120 miles, with the hospital located approximately in the center.)

These are just two examples of new and expanded services we implemented, which ranged from providing athletic trainers to area high schools, to developing programs for seniors throughout our service area, to implementing a back-pack program for underprivileged children, to a friends' club membership program—to name a few examples.

Obviously, not every citizen in our market area chose to receive services from our facilities. Our hypothesis assumed some of these individuals would participate in these outreach services, *i.e.,* have a good experience, and then choose our facility the next time their family required more intensive services, i.e., a medical clinic visit, hospitalization, or joint replacement surgery.

For example, perhaps a family's first exposure to our health system occurred when their athlete son or daughter received services from our athletic trainer in their local high school. This is why every consumer contact needed to be a great experience, so they would return for other services. Thus, *you never know what will ring the bell.*

This became an important slogan, which we found to be true based on market share data. Many of these new programs and services were started with limited resources, growing to the point of commanding dedicated resources complementary of their growth. To describe the interconnectivity of our services throughout our market, I ask you to envision a large net covering a significant corner of the state. The knots represent the various services tied to representative communities, and the cords of the net represent the interconnectivity of the services within the system. I believe this philosophy will serve well, (1) the people you have been called to serve, (2) the communities embellished with your services, (3) your staff of servant leaders, and (4) your organization.

Inspiring, loving, servant leaders and staff make these growth-related initiatives come together and work well together on behalf of those you have been called to serve. The *Spark* becomes a *Flame. Growth is always good.*

7) *Always strive to make the pie larger, so everyone's piece will also be larger.*

Early in my career as a CEO, several community service agencies and our hospital were striving to provide what we referred to as seamless services throughout a large, shared service area. History had not always served these agencies well, in terms of their ability to work together collaboratively.

Jean Sturtevant, the regional director of these community-based services, and I agreed to collaborate in bringing the agency directors and the hospital together. We were both fairly new in our positions when we forged our agreement to improve these working relationships. This effort was founded and nurtured on the basis of the collaborative example Jean and I had established. Jean, who is on my list of mentors, is a remarkable individual who I learned a great deal from during these processes.

In an effort to provide outside third-party facilitation, we retained the services of a futurist from the southeastern portion of the United States. He met with this large group onsite several times over a period of six months. I, along with Jean and others, found his approach unique and exactly what we needed to rekindle and recommit to these working relationships.

As our consultant helped us identify the underlying issues and begin to strengthen our working relationships, I took special note of one of his several admonishments to the group. He said, "We should collectively focus on making the pie larger, so everyone's individual piece would be larger." He said this should clearly be our objective— rather than harboring competitive instincts and doing the things we had been doing to not only protect, but to enlarge our individual pieces of the pie, at the expense of the whole pie. This struck a chord with everyone present that day. This mantra became the platform on which we rebuilt our collaborative relationships.

This change of focus was not only instrumental for this group, as I have found it applicable in many situations. It applies to our own organizations and to the discussion we had in the previous section. As the organization grows vertically and horizontally, everyone's contribution as a *piece* of the ownership, becomes larger. *Growth is always good.*

8) *Skate to where the puck is going to be and not where it is.*
I will join the ranks of those who have been accused of either overusing and/or misusing the quote originally credited to Walter Gretzky and passed on to the world through his son, Wayne Gretzky, renowned hockey player. You will note I have modified it a bit from the original, "Skate to where the *puck is going, not where it has been.*"

Admittedly, I am not a hockey fan, but I am a staunch fan of this quote. I do find more applicability in my version, *"Skate to where the puck is going to be, not where it is."*

My application pertains to creating an inspiring, loving, servant leader culture and anticipating, (1) the future needs of those we have been called to serve, (2) where our industry is going, (3) our future capacity as an organization, (4) what the political climate will be, (5) where the growth opportunities are the greatest, and (6) future financial requirements and benefits—and then skating, (or mobilizing resources) to where this *collective puck* is going to be—to where our dreams will lead us.

Other than learning from our past (or where the puck has been), little is to be gained in skating to where the puck has been. With the warp speed in which our internal and external environments change, the puck will have moved by the time we skate to where the puck is; hence, we need to skate to where the puck is going to be.

As I utilize this quote to illustrate plans and strategy, it is always based on the immense positive capacity of an inspiring, loving, servant leader culture, as a given; and intentional growth is made possible only through such cultures and organizations. *Growth is always good.*

9) *Proceed until apprehended.*
    Over ten years ago, I had the privilege of becoming acquainted with and working with Mr. Joe Tye, CEO and Head Coach of Values Coach, Inc. Among other good works, Joe is credited with the phrase, "Proceed until apprehended."

    I have come to appreciate this phrase a great deal as I view it as a positive outcome produced by cultures characterized as inspiring, loving, servant leader cultures. This is also characteristic of these cultures and organizations that have become more nimble by entrusting their staff members, as servant leaders, to make timely decisions and do the right things. *Growth is always good.*

10) *No Need to Own Everything; Just Need Access*
    For most of my life, I had subscribed to a possessive belief that ownership was the most effective means of promulgating growth and experiencing success. Through my emphasis on building collaborative relationships in recent years, I have come to believe we do not need to own everything, as long as we have access to required resources or services through renting, leasing, exchanging, or sharing required resources.

    One of our neighbors back on the farm was a successful farmer—and a colorful individual. He often remarked, with a grin, "I do not want to farm all of the land in the county, just the land that adjoins the land I currently farm." He did not say he wanted to *own* all of the land; he only wanted to *farm* all of the land that adjoined the land he currently farmed.

In some circumstances, it is better not to own for financial reasons. In other situations, insisting on ownership may hamper our ability to respond to timely opportunities. I stand by my convictions, (1) good things *fall out* of collaborative relationships and (2) we should focus on making the pie larger, so everyone's piece is larger. These are the outcomes when we are committed to working together. The inherent spirit associated with inspiring, loving, servant leadership seeks these types of relationships.

I believe the following scenario *generally* depicts a progressive, cyclic chain of events:

Tendencies; Not Assurances:

Timely Decisions *provide* Opportunities;
Opportunities *promote* Growth;
Growth *produces* Financial Gains;
Financial Gains *result in stability and stimulate* Growth; and
Growth *provides more* Opportunities.
Growth is always good.

Motivation (fear-based) Scatters. Inspiration (love-based) Gathers.

32) Celebrate, Celebrate, Celebrate

Inspiring, loving, servant leader cultures usually have a great deal to celebrate, as they should. This is analogous to happy, joyful, closely-knit families who uphold formal and informal family gatherings as important, and at times, almost ritualistic in nature. We can describe this as a culture they have created within and specifically for their family. For some families, this culture may also be heritage-based and consistently traditional with long-standing occasions and celebrations.

For many of us, observing the happiness, caring, and sharing these family members have for their family and one for another promotes an envious state of mind. Similarly, employees trapped in uninspiring organizations often gaze upon their counterparts in happy, caring, and sharing cultures within other organizations, and for many, these observations also lead to an envious state of mind.

As we have discussed, inspiring, loving, servant leader organizations focus on organizational dreams and promote and support the personal dreams of their employees. The fulfillment and realization of dreams at any level calls for celebrations that recognize and honor individuals, concerted team efforts, and individual and organizational accomplishments. Celebrations contribute to the renewal and affirmation of collaborative relationships and accomplishments.

1) *Honor and uphold the history and culture of the organization—and celebrate these whenever possible.*
   Most organizations, like families, have long-standing histories and cultures. Such histories and cultures serve as both *anchors* and *sails* for their respective organizations. The *anchor* allows the organization to maintain a connecting chain, a lifeline tied to its origin, reflecting its reason for existence, serving as an accounting of its growth and survival, and providing a sense of pride, confidence, and security. The anchor keeps the vessel, the organization, from drifting away from the purpose, principles, and values on which it was founded.

   The *sails*, via the rigging (the system of ropes, cables, and chains), allow the vessel, the organization, to move forward in various directions and at variable speeds; thus, representing the hopes, dreams, and destinies of the future. It too, provides a spirit of pride and accomplishment—and confidence in traversing the future and the unknown.

It is important for us to talk about, reflect upon, share, and celebrate our organizational histories and culture; not only for preserving the past, but for instilling trust and confidence in the future of the culture and the organization. After all, *we become what we think about, talk about, dream about, and profess to be important.*

As someone newer to the organization and the community, I have often taken the opportunity to publicly express my gratitude for all of those who have gone before me in establishing the organization and culture; which in turn, has provided the opportunity for me to serve the organization. We need to be respectful and appreciative of the pride most communities have for these organizations.

2) *Celebrate individual, departmental, team, and organizational-wide dreams and accomplishments.*
Inspiring, loving, servant organizations tend to have a great deal to celebrate. This is true for a variety of reasons. When we have an organization full of (informal and formal) servant leaders, facilitators, ambassadors, specialists, caring volunteers, and creative thinkers who are all *proceeding until apprehended,* there are many dreams being realized and accomplishments taking place. There is a great deal to celebrate—working together and celebrating together are integrated processes.

This is good and the way it should be. This is all about employees being creative, trusted, and encouraged to build collaborative relationships among themselves and with outside organizations. *Good things fall out of good relationships—and relationships move at the speed of trust.*

3) *Recognize Special/Unique Events*
Birthdays:
Each of us has something unique to celebrate at least one

time per year—our birthday. This is an opportunity to recognize each of our most important assets on an annual basis. Many of us joke about getting older, approaching and/or going over the hill, or not getting any younger; yet, most of us appreciate having our birthdays acknowledged.

Recognizing birthdays is a respectful thing to do, but recognizing birthdays needs to be done respectfully. There is a variety of initiatives that organizations have chosen to recognize (and celebrate) employee birthdays. The various options will be determined by inspiring, loving, servant leaders within your organization.

Employees need to have the opportunity to opt out of any type of birthday recognition. Most employees are comfortable with their name and the *birth date* of the specific month being shared; however, I recommend never listing the year during which employees were born—under *any* circumstances. I recommend you sponsor a birthday recognition program for everyone in your organization. The management team will discover gratification, and the employees will experience satisfaction.

Service Recognition:

Every employee has another unique day each year—their first day with the organization. Even though it occurs each year they are employed, it is generally celebrated incrementally, i.e., every five years is fairly typical. The details will be designed by and specifically on behalf of the organization.

I am a strong proponent of employee service recognition programs and associated awards. I always advocate that this is an excellent opportunity to *celebrate life and honor service.* I recommend that detailed planning will call for at least one guest invitation, a relaxing and inviting venue, special dinner menu selections, entertainment, and generous awards to commemorate the years of service being honored.

Service recognition is a wonderful opportunity for the employee's supervisor to speak on their behalf. It is also fitting for the CEO and other leadership team members to share prepared remarks commemorating the event and recognizing those being honored. It is also a great opportunity to express appreciation to family members for the support they provide to the employees. Collectively, all of these activities are characteristic of an inspiring, loving, servant leader organization.

4) *As a Last Resort*

I believe celebrations are a significant component of inspiring, loving, servant leader organizations and corresponding cultures. As such, I believe your organizations will have a significant number of dreams and accomplishments to celebrate throughout the year.

If you believe you need to sponsor more celebrations and nothing comes to mind, just do the next best thing and make something up. *Breaking bread together* always adds a special touch to any social activity. I am a strong advocate of providing refreshments. This is a personal carry-over from my days growing up on the farm. My mother and grandmother, in addition to the other farm ladies in our little rural neighborhood, would predictably provide refreshments for all visitors—planned and unplanned alike.

Motivation (fear-based) Scatters. Inspiration (love-based) Gathers.

LIGHTING THE TORCH... INSPIRE THE WORLD

This chapter, which includes eight practical suggestions and recommendations, will prove helpful in positioning your organization as a humble, shining example of how an organization comprised of inspiring, loving, servant leaders (formal and informal) treats its employees; fulfills personal and organizational dreams; functions as a strong, engaged corporate citizen; and returns more to the world than it extracts.

1) **Organization as a Strong Corporate Citizen**

In the previous chapter, "The Flame . . . Inspire Others," I included the following paragraphs:

As the CEO and leadership team, it is important to inspire the entire organization to be a strong corporate citizen. In many communities, the organization you represent may be one of the largest, if not the largest company in your community or communities. In turn, many of your employees are residents of the communities you serve and represent.

I introduce this in this chapter, "Fanning the Flame

. . . Inspire Others," as this initiative sends an important message to employees you not only care about them, but you care about their families, and the community or communities in which they live. Building and promoting the organization as a strong corporate citizen is an opportunity to collectively live and demonstrate inspiring, loving, servant leadership on a grander scale. This will be discussed in more detail in the next chapter, "Lighting: The Torch . . . Inspire the World."

The CEO and leadership team are primarily responsible for creating and positioning the organization as a strong corporate citizen. Within inspiring, loving, servant leader cultures, this naturally becomes a large-team sport with many opportunities for all staff participation. Becoming a strong corporate citizen will be accomplished through representation in collaborative relationships with school systems, churches, service organizations, chambers of commerce, other corporations, professional associations, and business-related networks comprised of similar organizations. These relationships provide excellent opportunities to match needs, interests, and talents.

Service clubs are predictably (1) interested in recruiting new members, and (2) seeking speakers for their meetings, which generally occur on a weekly basis. These provide excellent opportunities to encourage employees to become members. Providing circuit speakers for the meetings is an excellent means of introducing new programs and services to the communities. It may not be necessary to organize a formal speakers bureau, but it is important to identify a host of individuals who enjoy presenting on specific topics and are comfortable serving as excellent ambassadors on behalf of the organization.

Most communities sponsor festivals, parades, or other traditional events throughout the year. I recommend your organization identify opportunities to participate in these community-sponsored events, which are generally laced with significant local community pride. The communities your organization serves will appreciate your assistance in the division of labors and mere representation, and your organization will be grateful for the opportunity to spread goodwill and make positive differences in the lives of others.

In most mature relationships, every effective interaction flows back and forth as a two-way street and is based on the premise of giving and taking. An effective mantra for your organization is to speak of your organization's desire to *not only be a taker, but also a giver*—and then believe it and act accordingly.

Motivation (fear-based) Scatters. Inspiration (love-based) Gathers.

2) Foster and Practice a Spirit of Hospitality

I am fond of the word, *hospitality*, which is defined as "the friendly and generous reception and entertainment of guests, visitors, or strangers." How could inspiring, loving, servant leader organizations not be hospitable, as defined? My answer is they cannot be anything but hospitable. As the saying goes, *It feels as American as baseball and apple pie.*

During my early years as a young executive at Bryan Memorial Hospital, I was the recipient of a hallmark hospitality experience, which has cemented my convictions:

We were in the process of replacing the radiographic equipment in one of our heart catherization labs. Through the evaluation and selection process, we had narrowed the field to two major vendors. One of the two contenders was General Electric (GE). During the process, GE privately informed us that they were in the process of producing a new radiographic concept and configuration, which would prove revolutionary to the industry. This obviously piqued our interest in learning more. The timing of this opportunity initially appeared good and not so good, simultaneously.

General Electric invited Jim Peter, director of cardiology services, and me to visit their production plant in Milwaukee, Wisconsin. It would not be the amount of the money they invested on our behalf; but the way they treated us that would make this a memorable experience—an example of *hospitality*.

Our itinerary called for us to fly to Milwaukee the first day, stay overnight, spend the next full day at the plant, and fly back late the evening of the second day. The GE account representative, Jim, and I were flown to Milwaukee in a company plane the afternoon of the first day. We were picked up by limousine and escorted to our hotel. After checking in, we were driven to a nice restaurant for dinner and back to our hotel for the night. The dinner and hotel accommodations were exceptional. *We were made to feel welcomed, valued, and treated as special guests.*

Since we had a full day scheduled at the plant on the second day, we got an early start with breakfast at the hotel. After breakfast, we were whisked off to the GE Production Plant by limousine, once again. As we arrived at the GE campus, I remember first being impressed with the enormous size of the facility and the extensive landscaping.

I will never forget how I felt when we veered slightly to the left, approaching the entrance to the GE campus. The large sign designating the General Electric company campus was impressive. What really caught our attention, however, were these words, emboldened in bright colors:

Welcome to:
Mr. Jim Peter and Mr. Roger Steinkruger
Bryan Memorial Hospital
Lincoln, Nebraska

Wow, they really knew how to make two young men from Nebraska feel welcomed. As Jim and I stepped out of the limousine into the fresh morning air, we did so with an extra spring of confidence and anticipation in our steps as we made our way to the front entrance. *We were made to feel welcomed, valued, and treated as special guests.*

This may have been the first gesture of hospitality and attention to detail for the day, but it certainly was not the last as the day unfolded. We were warmly greeted at the front entrance by a customer service representative who led us directly to an adjoining conference room. Waiting our arrival in the conference room were the division vice president, the manager, and the entire team responsible for the design and construction of the new radiographic heart catheterization system.

No one arrived late or left the meeting early; and by the way they interacted amongst themselves and with us, it appeared this meeting was the first priority of the day—and they enjoyed their work. Of special note: Remember what I had shared previously about food being a social element? There it was, a continental breakfast buffet set before us. *We were made to feel welcomed, valued, and treated as special guests.*

It was now time to get down to business. After the customary exchange of welcome statements and introductions, the vice president set the tone by *affirming their appreciation to us for taking time to spend the day with them.* This was an interesting twist. He continued by explaining that we were the first individuals to not only see the prototype, but to lay-hands on it, manipulate it, and put it through the rigors. They would be indebted to us for our feedback. This was Jim's forte, as a knowledgeable and technical individual who could match function with clinical needs.

Before relinquishing to the manager and team, the vice president concluded his brief remarks with (1) his respectful acknowledgement and appreciation of the manager and team, (2) an outline of the itinerary for the day, (3) a tactful explanation of their request for both of us to sign Confidentiality/

Non-disclosure Statements, and (4) a reaffirmation of how much they appreciated our visit and evaluation of the system. For us, he had affirmed this unique opportunity for two young men from Lincoln, Nebraska, to provide pre-market feedback on a major General Electric product. *We were made to feel welcomed, valued, and treated as special guests.*

This would be remembered as a great day—and the first day to building a collaborative relationship that would last for years to come. *Good things fall out of good relationships.* I will always remember being ushered into the mocked-up heart catheterization room secured with solid walls, no windows, and electronically-controlled locks. In the middle of the room was a canvas-draped structure, presumably the prototype.

When unveiled, I was surprised to see a rather crude; but yet highly-sophisticated, fully-operational radiographic system with multiple cables and wires supporting the new revolutionary C-arm (attaching the x-ray tube at the opening of the "C," replacing the traditional overhead x-ray tube).

Jim was invited to manipulate and operate the system. From this, he provided several much-appreciated suggestions, which made their way into the final design. Without comment at the time, we both understood why this experience was being treated with utmost emphasis on the confidentiality associated with trade secrets. *We were made to feel welcomed, valued, and treated as special guests.*

Jim and I returned to work the next day, eager to share our observations and recommendations for our next steps. Within three weeks, we finalized system/purchase details, reached agreement on a delivery/installation plan, finalized the terms of the purchase agreement, and issued the purchase order for the very first C-arm system to roll off of GE's assembly line.

Consequently, we were the first hospital in the world to not only purchase, but to install the new system. Our hospital and newly-designed/constructed heart catheterization lab and staff were featured in GE's glossy promotional materials. We were honored to demonstrate our system to groups from countries around the world. (I still have a business card from the Japanese representatives.) Predictably, these experiences became fewer and fewer within the next six to twelve months, as other hospitals purchased the system.

Motivation (fear-based) Scatters. Inspiration (love-based) Gathers.

3) Establish a Welcome Board—Mean It, Speak It, and Live It

I devoted significant white space in sharing the above experience with General Electric for two reasons. *First*, this experience reaffirms several principles I have specifically discussed in previous sections; some of which are directly related to *hospitality*.

Second, I am thankful to have had this experience early in my career. To this day, I not only remember the activities of these two days; but, more importantly, I distinctly remember how I was made to feel—and how recalling the experience makes me feel even today. This is an example of *emotion trumping memory*.

One thing we adopted shortly after our visit to the General Electric plant was implementation of a *Welcome Board*. We have continued to employ this initiative since that time. If you are not currently doing something like this, I encourage you to consider doing so.

We have never had anything as elaborate as General Electric's marquee on their sign identifying their campus. Over the years, we have progressed from a hand-written welcome sign posted on a pedestal sign—to a computer-generated, large print version, still posted on a pedestal sign. The latter, which measures approximately 12in. x 18in., appears more professional and is easy to manage on a daily basis. The ideal location for this welcome board is inside the front entrance of your facilities. We simply posted the names of the individuals and their respective agencies or organizations under the standing *"Welcome to."*

These are the associated benefits of providing such a welcome board:

Internal Benefits: (The Torch . . . Inspiring the World through Staff)

1) This practice models messaging with staff in welcoming visitors as special guests. Inspired and loving employees are proud of their organization; and in turn, take pride in being hospitable and making your guests feel at home.

2) The welcome board is a means of demonstrating transparency with the staff. Staff appreciate knowing what is going on within the organization. In conjunction to making our guests feel welcome, we often tour these same individuals and groups of individuals throughout the facility. It is helpful for staff to be aware when we have guests within the facility, as some even take the opportunity to personally add their greetings.

3) It is helpful for the receptionist stationed near the front entrance to be able to anticipate someone's arrival. This provides the receptionist with an extra edge in making our guests feel welcomed and special.

4) All staff are encouraged to inform the administrative assistant when they are expecting guests, so no one goes unnoticed as a special visitor. This also conveys an important message to staff that we appreciate them and the role they play as ambassadors, on behalf of the organization.

   The keeper of the welcome board was inspired to add this important mantra at the bottom of each welcome sign, which reads, *"Arrive as a guest; leave as a friend."* This reflects the experience we intend for all those who grace us with their presence.

1) Most everyone is touched with a warm feeling within, when they see their names lifted up in print on a welcome board, regardless of size or design. *They are made to feel welcomed, valued, and treated as a special guest.*

2) For many coming through our front entrances, this will be their first contact, of any kind, with the organization. This may be the first time they have visited the community. For others, this will be the first time they have been in our facility. The receptionist may be the first person they interact with as an ambassador of the organization.

   For these individuals, the welcome board is the *first point of contact,* even before being greeted by the receptionist. I contend the receptionist is the one person who frames a visitor's first and last (ing) impression, as they enter and exit the facility. The welcome board sets the tone and makes the receptionist's work easier; not only for first-time visitors, but for all visitors.

   The best complement to the effectiveness of one strategically placed pedestal welcome board, is to have 250 (an arbitrary number of employees) mobile welcome boards roaming throughout our facilities; all of whom exude the spirit of inspiring, loving, servant leaders, as evidenced through their smiles, greetings, and offers to assist.

3) I contend most of us confirm our *first* impressions of an organization within the *first* ten minutes after passing through the front entrance. I cannot begin to estimate how long it takes to reverse a *bad* first impression, but I believe it may be measured in months or even years, if at all. It makes *sense* and *cents* to invest in making and maintaining commendable first impressions. We do this by creating inspiring, loving, servant leader cultures and associated organizations.

I am reminded of two premises we have established previously, (1) we only have one opportunity to make a good first impression, and (2) if each of us is in a position to influence 250 people, positively (or negatively), imagine what 250 inspired, loving, servant leaders, as *torches*, can do to inspire their little corner of the world. The numbers become staggering: 250 x 250 = 62,500 potentially positive (or negative) personal contacts.

4) The welcome board is only an adjunct to the creation of an inspiring, loving, servant leader culture. We have received an extraordinary amount of positive feedback regarding the welcome board. When our honored guests prepare to exit the facility, we make a point of walking with them to the front entrance. As a final gesture of goodwill and best wishes, we remove their welcome sign, give it to them, and express our appreciation for their visit.

During subsequent conversations, these individuals often relay that they have posted the signs in their offices and shared these with their peers, or have taken the signs home to share with their families. Invariably, they will add something to the effect of, "I really appreciated the welcome sign; it made me feel special." Purpose and mission accomplished.

Motivation (fear-based) Scatters. Inspiration (love-based) Gathers.

4) Organization as a Community Asset and Strong Corporate Citizen

Regardless of the official type of ownership, I recommend you view, create, and promote your organizations not only as community assets, but also as strong corporate citizens. Some of your organizations are publicly-owned, others are privately-held corporations, some are publicly traded companies, and still others are nonprofit corporations. My comments relate to all organizations.

If your organization subscribes to *never doing anything illegal, unethical, or immoral,* I presume you qualify as a community asset and your community views you accordingly. The organization, or at least your facility, is located in a community where your staff work, play, and worship. This may qualify your organization as a community asset, but not necessarily a strong corporate citizen.

I liken what the inspiring, loving, servant leader is to the organization; to what the inspiring, loving, servant leader organization (as a strong corporate citizen) is to the community—or communities they serve, their little corner of the world.

Inspiring Individual/Organization = Inspiring Organization/Community. As *individuals,* we are not only judged by how we treat others, but also on how we conduct business; as *organizations,* we are not only judged by how we treat others, but also on how we conduct business.

Strong corporate citizen organizations are not just *takers*; more importantly, they are also *givers.* I contend your company cannot become the strong corporate citizen I envision unless it is first a culture, an organization bustling at the seams, with inspiring, loving, servant leaders (formal and informal). If you want to become a strong corporate citizen, *turn to* your inspired employees—and then, *turn them loose.*

Motivation (fear-based) Scatters. Inspiration (love-based) Gathers.

5) **Entertain and Make People Comfortable in Your Home**

This may be easier for some organizations to master than others. I will speak from a hospital's perspective, but I believe similar opportunities exist for other entities. Some would say this may be harder for hospitals, since many people associate their aversion to needles and other invasive equipment(s) with hospitals. Even though our organization was a nonprofit, 501-C corporation, we promoted our hospital as theoretically belonging to the communities, those we have been called to serve.

We have always maintained it is important to provide an inspiring, loving, servant atmosphere, so people will become comfortable visiting the hospital for a wide variety of reasons. With respect to providing care, we never wish for anyone to be sick or injured. Our objective is to provide excellent care and maintain a stellar reputation, so when individuals have healthcare needs, they will hopefully choose our facility. Beyond direct patient care, we wanted to provide a wide variety of reasons for people to pass through our doors, taking advantage of our services and our hospitality.

Service organizations, particularly in smaller communities, are often looking for locations to conduct meetings, many on a weekly basis. We provided a conference room for a Kiwanis Club to meet weekly during the lunch hour. This was a symbiotic relationship, as the club had a nice place to meet over lunch and the hospital cafeteria benefited from the additional revenue. Such service organizations are generally seeking presenters. Since the hospital always has a variety of new and existing services and programs to discuss, this provided an excellent opportunity to promote our services. Having these meetings onsite also made it convenient for several of our staff to attend meetings, as members of the club. I speak not only as a member, but also as the club's president for two consecutive terms.

The Kiwanis Club was only one example where we opened our conference rooms to other outside organizations. Being centrally-located in the county and having food services available provided an attractive option for several other community and non-profit organizations to meet. This was just one way to give back to the communities we served.

Working with surrounding school systems, we provided a variety of onsite health educational experiences. We also sponsored "Lunch and Learns," which were targeted for the public. These combined complimentary lunches with health-related presentations and discussions. As a member of *Sterling Connections,* a hospital friends membership club, one could stop by the hospital at any time without an appointment, and have their blood pressure checked and ask health-related questions free of charge. These are a few examples of initiatives that provided opportunities for community members to become familiar and comfortable with us through more causal settings—and to give back to the communities we were called to serve.

Motivation (fear-based) Scatters. Inspiration (love-based) Gathers.

6) Media as Friend and Not Foe

We should view the media as a friend and not a foe. As we strive to be a *Torch*, a light to the world (at least our little corner of the world), this admonishment is important to heed, individually and organizationally. A prerequisite for developing such a relationship with the media is to foster a servant leader culture which models this symbolic torch sharing its light with many.

Assuming we have met the above prerequisite, there are additional steps which will move us to this desired state. We must believe and accept (1) the media's work is important to society, (2) building collaborative relationships with the media is possible, (3) the media can be instrumental in telling our stories, (4) playing offense is more effective than playing defense, and (5) we can make each other's work easier and more effective, through collaborative relationships. *Relationships move at the speed of trust.*

Inspiring, loving, servant leader organizations have a great deal to talk about, within and outside the walls of their facilities. On the list are human interest stories, staff promotions, individual and organizational dreams come true, community service spots, new services and programs, educational offerings, new collaborative relationships, existing service updates, new technologies, and others yet to be inspired.

Media sources are generally interested in such offerings, so the development of trusting, collaborative relationships is beneficial to both parties. Do not be bashful about scheduling a luncheon meeting with the media's representatives and your leadership team at your facility to address these and other issues of your choosing. Be sure to include the names and respective media agencies of you guests on your welcome board. Depending on the number of agencies, you may choose to repeat this in two or more luncheon meetings. These meetings will provide an excellent opportunity for you to control the message by providing an operational overview, answering questions, and touring your facilities.

Predictably, they will sense something different about your inspiring, loving, servant leader organization. This is a good time to remember, *Words tell, but passion sells.* Together, you will likely identify items for follow up stories. They will be appreciative of your invitation and the time spent with your team and the organization. *Good things fall out of good relationships.*

Motivation (fear-based) Scatters. Inspiration (love-based) Gathers.

7) **Tell the Organization's Story; Then Tell It Again and Again**
We have discussed the importance of writing the organization's story in previous segments. In this section, emphasis remains on not only writing the story, but on telling it again and again, in a variety of afforded settings. This is important, as an inspiring, loving, servant leadership culture, you will always have a great deal to write about and tell about.

Repetition is good and generally improves the effectiveness of the story. Telling and hearing something in a repetitive, but appropriate fashion, cements the message in our minds; other team members; and those we are interacting with at the time. You will know *the juice has been worth the squeeze* when you overhear members of the leadership team, other managers, and staff members sharing *the story* with others, almost verbatim to how you have *rolled it out* many times.

To support my claim, I will take you back to my elementary school years. I was blessed to attend a one-room country school from kindergarten through eighth grade. The entire school was only approximately 24ft. x 40ft. or about 960 sq. ft. The highest number of students I recall during my school years was twelve, representing nine grades.

Throughout the day, the teacher conducted classes for each grade and each class, with students and teacher positioned together around a small table at the front of the room. The remaining students were expected to be studying while the teacher was conducting classes. You can imagine how difficult it was to study without involving oneself in the class instruction taking place at the front of the room.

I have often mused the thing that helped me graduate eighth grade was, *"By the time I graduated eighth grade, I had been through seventh grade, eight times; sixth grade, seven times; fifth grade, six times; fourth grade, five times; and so on down through the remaining grades; you see the picture and get the point."* Even though I have fun sharing this, there is a serious note about the positive effects associated with repetition. The combination of repetition and my opportunities to mentor younger students, provided excellent educational experiences during my elementary years.

Repetition of the message and *mentoring of others* are both important in sharing and modeling the essence of our organizational stories.

Motivation (fear-based) Scatters. Inspiration (love-based) Gathers.

8) Celebrate Your Story with Friends Outside of Organization

In the previous chapter, "Fanning the Flame. . .Inspire Others", we discussed the importance of celebrating dreams realized and accomplishments noted within our organizations. We not only have an inherent need to celebrate within our immediate family, we also have a similar need to celebrate with our extended family members.

When we personally feel and experience the internal benefits of working in inspiring, loving, servant organizations, we want to share; to encourage; to further inspire; and to celebrate with others outside of our organization. This is one way we can be *Torches . . . Inspiring the World;* at least our little corner of the world.

The list of things to celebrate is proportionate to the unlimited number of realized dreams and accomplishments. This is specific to the individual organizations. I will continue to attest to the importance of celebrating our history, our culture, our dreams, our accomplishments, and our aspirations for the future.

Motivation (fear-based) Scatters. Inspiration (love-based) Gathers.

REFUELING THE SOULS AND ORGANIZATIONS OF THE WORLD

In Conclusion: "The Last of the Good Will Be Better and The First of the Better Will Inspire to Be Best."

I had been preparing this manuscript over a period of several months. During the third week of May, 2020, as I approached completion of the first draft, I paused briefly to reflect on how different the world is today, compared to one year ago, six months ago; and yes, to only four months ago.

The coronavirus, only visible through intense magnification, has brought the world, our country, our state, and our city to their knees. Like many of you, I never envisioned witnessing such devastation during my lifetime. I find myself reminded of one of my own admonishments, *"There is always a little good in what appears to be the worst at the time."*

Through self-reflection, I have completed due diligence in asking myself: "Have the effects of this invisible enemy changed my overall outlook, my personal convictions, any of my views and opinions shared in this manuscript, or morphed any of the things I have learned experientially during my lifetime?" To the contrary, I believe our current and future societal circumstances affirm an even greater need for these essential tenets I've expressed in this book.

I have referenced Lance Secretan's work on several occasions throughout this book. These references characterize my respect for Lance and his many fine works. If Lance only allowed me *one takeaway* from everything he has written about and/or spoken to, his distinction between motivation and inspiration would be my cherished treasure: *Motivation* is "lighting a fire *under* someone" and *Inspiration* is "lighting a fire *within* someone."

The first time I heard Lance speak to this distinction, I remember his comment regarding motivation when he said, to the effect: "There is a place for motivation. If a fire breaks out in this room (the room in which he was speaking at the time) and someone yells, *'Fire! Fire! Get out of the room!,'* this would be a good use of such *motivation.*"

To provide credence to Lance's fine work built around these two premises, I recommend you turn to Lance's book, *"The Spark, the Flame, and the Torch . . . Inspire Self. Inspire Others. Inspire the World."*

Lance and I had shared a personal conversation during the early part of March, 2020. One of the topics of discussion at the time centered on early circumstances surrounding the coronavirus. In a follow-up text message to Lance a few days later on March 15, 2020. I shared this in my text: "Lance, it occurred to me, we are experiencing MOTIVATION on a scale this world has never seen before—and it is going to require INSPIRATION to bring everything back together again, like we have never before even imagined!" (emphasis added)

There is always a little good in what appears to be the worst at the time. During my lifetime, this global pandemic is absolutely *the worst of human conditions* I have experienced. Simultaneously, we do not need to look beyond our neighborhoods, our cities, our states, our country, and other countries throughout the world, to witness the best of human conditions and be inspired and displayed each and every day. *Interesting: Finding so much good in the midst of so much bad.* The words, *inspiring, loving,* and *servants* come to mind as I describe all of this good being shared these days.

All of the tenets upon which my writings are grounded, some more directly than others, are based on and emanate from the word *inspiration* or, as Lance reminds us, *lighting a fire within ourselves and others.* I do not profess promotion of a new-fangled management program or system.

Like the coronavirus, the far-reaching inspiration we are observing these days knows no geographical boundaries and does not discriminate on the basis of ethnicity, race, religion, profession, rank, income, or social status. The title of my book is the point, "Inspiration Universal and Unlimited . . . *Motivation Scatters. Inspiration Gathers.*"

As we plan for returning to our places of employment, one of our greatest fears is taking the coronavirus back to work with us. Even though this is of great concern, I am confident we will figure out how to accomplish both, returning to work and minimizing opportunity for infection or reinfection.

One of the things I pray we will take back to work with us is everything we will have learned about inspiring, loving, and serving others. Everyone old enough to remember these horrific days has the capacity to also recognize and remember all of the wholesome, happy, joyful, inspiring, loving, and caring gestures shared through the hands, hearts, and souls of servants.

These are several observations and admonishments, I leave with each of you:

1) We have all personally experienced a time-out hiatus, separating the way we were from the way we are—and the way we will be in the future. This is a great time for self-reflection, reassessment, and new convictions—a rebooting or a retooling, of sorts—in both our professional and personal lives.

    We are being called upon to cast out some of the old and create new things, new approaches to how and where we will work and play. These dynamics do not diminish the need for inspiring, loving, servant leadership, but actually enhance it through new expectations of leaders in all types of business, industry, and service organizations.

2) I encourage each of us to return to work as a more patient, inspiring, loving individual with the heart of a servant. Staff will be looking to us, as leaders, for a variety of new supportive measures centering on where they will be located, the tools they will need to perform their work, and the inspired disciplines necessary to be effective and successful in this new world of work. It will be important for us to turn to staff for their most creative ideas, suggestions, and recommendations in making these transitions as seamless and nondisruptive as possible.

   We will need to be mindful of, not only the work-related challenges, but also the family related changes employees will be juggling on a daily basis. This is a critical time for us to be supportive of the *employee-centered, family-focused* emphasis we discussed previously.

3) *To the CEO, the executive on a leadership team, the director, the manager, or the supervisor who has been less than encouraging, inspiring, loving, and has not practiced servant leadership,* I ask you to return to work with new convictions to believe in and emulate these traits and behaviors.

   Like your staff, you have been immersed in example after example of individuals at their best during these worst of times. You can go back a different leader. Since all of us have experienced the same conditions, the distinction will be noticeable, but you will not be chastised for the old you to the same extent—because we have all undergone a morphing, so to speak. The staff will be expecting a new you—a different leader. Being gracious and humble, with a little pinch of humor, will make everyone's return to work easier and more gratifying for you, the new inspiring, loving, servant leader.

4) *To the CEO, the executive on a leadership team, the director, the manager, or the supervisor who has believed in the enumerable*

benefits of inspiring, loving, servant leadership, but has not been confident enough or brave enough to be such in the midst of non-believers, I ask you to return to work with your spiritual armor strapped on and fully in place in the spirit of Ephesians 6.

Now will be the easiest time to make the change, because we have all shared the same experiences and noted all of the inspirational modeling taking place around us. Besides, it will be easier to enlist the support of others who also desire to be more inspiring, loving, servant leaders. The staff will be expecting a new you—the leader you have always wanted to be.

5) *To the CEO, the executive on a leadership team, the director, the manager, or the supervisor, who openly practices inspiring, loving, servant leadership, I say "Congratulations, way to go! I am confident I could learn from each of you."* I encourage you to return to work more emboldened than you were when you left, prior to the pandemic. You will return to work knowing the task ahead of you, though difficult, will be much easier because you are returning to a team of experienced inspiring, loving, servant leaders (informal and formal).

6) *To the individual who aspires to be a CEO, an executive on a leadership team, a director, a manager, or a supervisor,* I ask you to return to work with a servant's heart, a heart that yearns to be inspired and to inspire, to be loved and to love, and not to be served, but to serve. Now is an excellent time for you to return with these expectations, as everyone has shared the worst of our times; but has also observed the best of our human conditions on display.

Remember, you do not need to be in a management role to be a servant leader, as everyone can be a servant leader. It is a great time to define the type of formal leader you will be one day. I encourage you to seek out formal leaders in organizations who subscribe to inspiring, loving, servant leadership. These individuals will be easy to identify and, as such, they will be pleased to reach over (over and not down) and support you in pursuit of your aspirations.

7) *To the staff person returning to work, if you know yourself as an inspiring, loving, servant leader,* return with a pronounced commitment to continue being the individual who strives to make positive differences in the lives of others and in your organization. You will remember the inspiration you experienced as you observed others being inspiring and loving, during these difficult times. The formal leaders, other staff you work with, and the entire organization need you to be the *Flame . . . Inspiring Others.*

8) *To the staff person returning to work, if you have recognized yourself as a cynical, unfriendly, self-serving, non-team player employee,* I encourage you to return as a different individual. I trust you have observed the many acts of kindness, inspiring and loving in nature, being modeled during this difficult time. More importantly, I hope you have personally felt the sensations of these inspiring, loving gestures shared freely with our fellow Americans.

   If you have, you will want to come back as a different employee. This will be the ideal time to make this commitment, as everyone has shared this common experience. If you sincerely desire to make this change, and your organization does not support such a culture, I suggest you seek an organization which will support your desire for a new work life—and most likely, a new life away from work.

9) *To the person who is seeking their first job or a change in employment,* I encourage you to seek a culture and an organization that subscribes to and practices inspiring, loving, servant leadership. For those of you seeking your first job, it is likely you may be also be establishing your own family. One of the most gratifying outcomes of family and work, is to be able to be the same person at home and at work. The inspiring, loving, servant leadership organizations place emphasis on being employee-centered and family-focused—and making family-life a priority.

As you interview with various organizations, you will be able to differentiate and evaluate their commitments to promoting inspiring, loving, servant leader cultures. I suggest, if given the opportunity to interview onsite, you will be able to determine whether or not the organization subscribes to this within the first thirty to forty-five minutes onsite. I suggest you prepare a list of questions, which will help you cement your final impressions. The tenets of inspiring, loving, servant leadership offered in this book will be helpful in crafting such questions.

10) *Now, I speak to all CEOs, executives on leadership teams, directors, managers, supervisors, and staff members, who collectively reflect the culture of your organizations.* I recommend each of you individually, and all of your collectively, return to work with a renewed sense of purpose, unity, kindness, devotion, and identity—to be held high above by each of you as inspiring, loving, servant leaders—for all to see, experience, and bear testimony. Let us be ***the Spark*** *that inspires ourselves;* ***the Flame*** *that inspires others; and* ***the Torch*** *that inspires the world* and lights the paths for others to follow, for generations to come.

The time is now and in the days and months to come. This evolution in our places of work will be easier to accomplish now than it has ever been before in the history of mankind. We have all shared common experiences and challenges brought about by the coronavirus, witnessed multiple examples of kindness, inspiration, love, and concern for one another, and subscribed to the mantra, *"We are all in this together."*

We are all in this together as individuals, as families, as a society—and soon, we will all be in this together in our places of work. Let us learn from the experiences we have shared, the modeling we have observed, and take advantage of this, the ideal time to evoke positive, inspirational changes in our work environments and our organizational cultures. *There is always a little good in what appears to be the worst at the time.*

"The Last of the Good Will Be Better and The First of the Better Will Inspire to Be Best."

The End.

Best Wishes and God's Blessings Always!
Thank you,

Roger W. Steinkruger

ABOUT THE AUTHOR

Roger W. Steinkruger, the eldest of four children, was born and raised on a farm in Franklin County in south-central Nebraska. He characterizes his early life as humble, simple, and wholesome. Roger takes pride in his early upbringing and is quick to credit these experiences as the bedrock to many of the practical suggestions and recommendations he discusses in *Inspiration Universal and Unlimited..... Motivation Scatters; Inspiration Gathers.*

His elementary education, grades K-8th grade, occurred in a one-room country schoolhouse. Described in a humorous manner, serious arguments are made for the virtues of these experiences in molding the author for a lifetime of inspirational, loving, servant leadership.

After graduating from Franklin High School, Roger attended the University of Nebraska at Lincoln, receiving a Bachelor's Degree in Economics and Management. This was followed with a Master's Degree in Public Administration Healthcare Emphasis from the University of Nebraska at Omaha.

The pinnacle of Roger's combined educational and work-related experiences is found in his work with Lance Secretan, PhD, internationally renowned author, speaker, consultant, and friend of the author. Roger is a graduate of the Higher Ground Leadership Retreat at the Secretan Center in Ontario, Canada, personally hosted by his mentor.

Roger was honored to write the foreword for Lance's latest book, *The Bellwether Effect…Stop Following. Start Inspiring!* This is one of the ways Roger describes his work with Lance, "Every time I interact with Lance, it is like going back to the well one more time for a drink of fresh water."

Roger's entire fifty-plus year career was devoted to healthcare supervision, management, and administration, with the last twenty-five years as a hospital CEO. He has experienced and addressed almost every conceivable work-related set of circumstances and challenges one can imagine. Most importantly, he has reaped the personal gratification that comes from devotion as an inspirational, loving, servant leader.

Although these occurred in healthcare settings, these lessons are applicable to all human interactions within our homes, places of work, and communities. Roger's wealth of knowledge and wisdom is tapped by an extensive intended audience. He reminds us that everyone is a leader—and everyone should strive to be the same person at home and at work. If you desire to become a more inspiring, loving, servant leader, this is the book for you. Leveraging Roger's practical suggestions and recommendations will plot your course and propel your journey, regardless of your current station in life.

www.ingramcontent.com/pod-product-compliance
Lightning Source LLC
Chambersburg PA
CBHW061432150726
47987CB00001B/179